'Noele's story reads almost like a modern morality play for twentieth-century parents, teachers, social workers, child psychiatrists, magistrates – in fact all those people whose lives bring them into authoritative proximity to emotionally deprived children. It takes courage to show one's private feelings in public, and I hope that Noele's courage in writing this story will encourage those of us who are part of "the system" to look critically yet again at it and ourselves.'

Bridget C. Downer, A.A.P.S.W.

CHILD OF A SYSTEM

NOELE ARDEN
Foreword by Dr Anthony Storr
Coda by Bridget C. Downer A.A.P.S.W.

QUARTET BOOKS LONDON

107378

First published by Quartet Books Limited 1977
A member of the Namara Group
27 Goodge Street, London W1P 1FD

ISBN 0 7043 2134 3

Typesetting by Bedford Typesetters Limited

Printed in Great Britain by litho at The Anchor Press Ltd
and bound by Wm Brendon & Son Ltd
both of Tiptree, Essex

For those who cannot speak for themselves

FOREWORD

Dr Anthony Storr, F.R.C.P., F.R.C.Psych.

Very few patients who are committed to Rampton or Moss Side special hospitals are sufficiently intelligent or articulate to record their experience. The rarity of this account, therefore, is one reason why it is important. There are many others. Noele Arden was abandoned by her father when she was nineteen months old, and, although looked after by her paternal grandmother for a short period, entered her first institution at the age of two and a half. From then on her loveless progress was by way of children's homes, a workhouse, remand home, approved school, adult mental hospital, to her final destination, Rampton, the special hospital designed for anti-social patients suffering from mental subnormality. Here she spent eight and a half years, enlivened only by a brief transfer to Moss Side, until her mother, perhaps feeling guilty at her early abandonment of her, finally obtained her release.

Children seem to be born with a built-in conviction that they have a right to be loved and nurtured by two parents; and if they are not, resent this deprivation of their birthright. Some become fearful and depressed, or solitary and withdrawn. Others, like Noele Arden, who are more robustly endowed, become violent and anti-social. Violent behaviour is still generally treated with punishment, and some of the punishments which Noele Arden received were savage, ranging from public caning to severe beating up by the nurses in Rampton. Whereas children who have been loved learn from even quite mild punishments, since they chiefly mind the temporary withdrawal of love by the adults on whom they are dependent, those who have not been loved react with increased resentment and violence. For they have no love to lose, no reason to regard any adult with anything except hatred.

Violence may also be the only way a child has of asserting itself, of making itself felt as a person. Neglected, unloved children are like oppressed minorities, whose only voice is violence. As the author writes: 'No one seemed to care. As long as you were no trouble, you were almost ignored.' But, every time she was violent, she was treated violently. 'We were supposed to be mentally deficient and not responsible for our actions, so we should have been helped, not ill-treated.' No wonder she attempted suicide.

This dreadful account refers to institutions of twenty years ago, and some improvement has taken place since then. But, as recurrent newspaper reports of conditions in mental institutions attest, enormously much more urgently requires to be done. I hope this book will speed reform. It is so obviously authentic that no one can any longer dismiss accusations of ill-treatment in hospital by the mentally ill and the mentally handicapped as being the product of their disordered imaginations.

What is remarkable is that Noele Arden has survived with enough of her personality intact to write this book and, with help, to make some sort of adult life for herself in the community. As she writes herself of her own predicament: 'To live without destroying yourself with hate is an achievement.'

My first memory of the unpleasantness that seemed to overshadow my childhood and beyond was approximately at the age of nineteen months. Of the somewhat stormy marriage of my parents I remember only an isolated incident: my father went out of my life. I recall dimly my mother with my brother, a baby of about nine months, tucked uncomfortably under one arm, while Mother's free arm was, like her tongue, hurling abuse at Father who was at the bottom of the stairs. I was in between both parents, not understanding what was going on. Father went, and neither my brother, whom we called Buster, nor I ever saw Father again. I learnt in adult life that he had died in 1940.

I think Mother must have been working, as she was a trained nurse, and I saw little of her and Buster. My father's mother looked after me. She was an old lady in a long dress, usually dark in colour. Why or how I came to be in a convent at about the age of two and a half I don't really know, but there I was, with dark faceless figures to care, or not to care, for me. I used to wet my bed, and along with other offenders would be hoisted out of bed and marched to the toilet late every night; but alas, there was that inevitable puddle in the bed every morning. The unpleasant ritual that followed was always the same.

We wet ones were herded to the bathroom, which contained several baths. They were filled with cold water and evil-smelling disinfectant, and into this we were put complete with the offending wet sheets and nightclothes. Then, shivering with cold – and, I'm sure, a certain amount of fear – we were told how evil we were, and how filthy, and we must ask for God's forgiveness.

There was a large garden to play in and my precious possessions were an old doll's pram with no bottom in it and an old rubber inflatable rubber duck, only it would not blow up. I loved these toys and had hours of fun with them. How long I was there I don't know, for my next memory is of a little village in Surrey where Buster and I were both at home with our mother.

Buster was about four and I would be about five and a half. Where those missing years went I can't remember. We had a golden cocker spaniel called Goldie and a little black cat called Currell who got me into a grand scrape. She got up on the roof and I thought she was stuck, so with Buster's help up I went after her. Much to my surprise the cat got down easily, but not me. There I was, perched by the chimney, too terrified to move. By this time several neighbours had gathered, some with ladders, but unfortunately none was long enough and I would not budge. Finally the fire engine came to the rescue. I wish they hadn't. My behind felt the back of the hairbrush which my mother was very good at handling, and did I scream! I think the whole neighbourhood must have heard.

Buster and I spent many happy hours on the common behind our house. I think the war must have started, as by this time soldiers and convoys started going through the village. This reminds me of one of the days Buster was missing. He had been given a trike by old Mr Tucker, and like 'Little Sir Echo' was always far away.

The day in question was panic. Buster had gone off early in the morning and it was now early evening and not a sign of him. The police were looking – neighbours, older children and anyone who passed by were asked if they had seen a little boy on a trike. I was shut up in the house and told not to move or else. Much later, a very tired Buster and a relieved but angry mother came home. Buster had followed the soldiers and was found miles away. He got a hiding all right, poor little devil!

I think Buster would be about five and me about six and a half when we got into a scrape with our local butcher. We had an old twin pram and spent many hours coming down the hill in it. Buster would be at one end and me at the other. We tried to steer it by hanging out on one side or the other, but one day we didn't do it very well. We crashed into the butcher's window. Fortunately the window didn't break, but the pram was taken off us. After that escapade Mother started taking us to work with her – a decision we all regretted later.

Mother was helping a hairdresser clean her home and salon and Buster and I were put in the attic playroom. That was fine for a while. Then, one day, everyone started shouting, looking at the water pipes and phoning plumbers. Buster and I wondered what all the excitement was about. We hadn't long to wait. Buster and I had turned the whole water system off and the hairdresser was in the middle of perming and washing and all the palaver that goes on in a hair salon. We copped it – tanned and banned again.

At weekends, Mother used to cycle with us both in a carrier on the back of her bike to London. We went to see an Aunt Dorothy. I remember very little of her, but do remember an occasion when we got lost in the fog in Windsor Park. Mother heard what she thought was a man coming. She was pleased as she thought to ask the way out. Going towards the 'cough' we were confronted with the biggest deer we had ever seen. It was this animal we had heard cough, and were we scared! We did finally find our way out.

We had trouble in the village, where the Stirt boys were the local bullies. They smashed up Buster's trike and threw stones at us, but I soon found a good defence. I had a really blood-curdling scream, and if those boys came within a yard of me, I'd scream. It never failed – someone would always come to the rescue.

This scream got me a hiding in London. Why we were there I don't know, or where we were going. Mother had us on a

London railway station. Then, to my horror, she went on the moving stairs, escalators as they are called. Buster was in the safety of my mother's arms. I was on my own two feet and did not like this nasty moving thing. So I screamed. There was pandemonium and the thing was stopped. They thought I'd caught my foot in it. Mother was red-faced and angry and gave Buster to a man to hold. She hoisted me up, and none too gently as I remember it gave me a well-aimed smack on my behind. I did not dare yell then. I'd pushed my luck far enough.

These are only isolated incidents. Much of my childhood is dim in my mind, owing to the electric treatment (ECT as they call it) that I received later in my childhood.

I do remember Buster and me being sent to a children's home in Alsford, Hants. Why Mother sent us I don't know or understand. The home was quite a large one to our young eyes, and Buster and I were separated, boys one side, girls the other. Even at meals boys and girls were separated, so Buster and I only saw each other occasionally. I must have been nearly seven, maybe a little more. Buster is eighteen months younger than me.

We only saw each other at playtime, when we could play together in a big field. There were older boys helping on the home farm. There were swings at the top of the field, and through a gate was the farmyard. There were cows, pigs and chickens, and a lovely big cart-horse. Some of the big boys also helped in the vegetable gardens, but I don't think they lived in this home.

It was at this time that we first noticed real signs of the war. There were occasional planes in the sky, and these caused great excitement, and then there was the sound of the sirens, and sometimes the sound of dull bangs similar to the sound of quarry-blasting. Whether it was guns or bombs we could only surmise. When the sirens went, we were herded into a low building with mattresses packed tightly together on the floor, the windows covered with brown sticky tape and heavily covered with big black blinds. This room was used as a dormitory. Apart from all these precautions, we saw little or nothing of the war while we were there. Our days seemed to be

4

spent playing. I cannot recall any schooling, but I expect there was some.

One incident is very prominent in my mind. There was a young man employed on the farm who gave us sweets, but he also used to put his hand in the little girls' knickers. We didn't say anything, although we somehow knew it was wrong – it was worth it for the sweets.

I can remember no more of this particular children's home.

The year must be the end of 1942. Buster and I are in yet another children's home in Harpenden, Herts. This was a much larger home than the previous one, but as before, boys were one side, girls the other. This home was divided into several large houses and we had women looking after the girls. At Harpenden a lot of social work and entertainment was laid on for the children. There was a big hall and this was used for entertainment. Plays were put on by the children themselves with the help of a very talented man. We called him Uncle Frank. I was hopeless, with no talent at all. I could not dance or sing, though I dearly wanted to be in one of the plays. To Buster the separation was awful. He hated it and used to creep out of his house and come across to where I was. Many a night they found him in my bed or under it. Buster told me only the other day how they used to march him back to his own house and the woman in charge used to pull his pants down, suspend him across her knee for a few minutes, then belt into him with the hairbrush. He said the suspense was worse than the hiding.

I was not a very popular child and can remember no special friends. Perhaps I was too naughty. Until coming to this home, I myself cannot remember seeing our mother since we left our home in Surrey, but Buster said she did visit once at the previous home. I do remember Mother visiting Harpenden. She arrived dressed in the uniform of the ATS. She bought us each a box of blown birds' eggs – it seemed an unusual gift but they were very pretty. Needless to say they did not last very long. Memory once more fades. I cannot remember her going, just that fleeting recall of seeing her.

The grounds at Harpenden were large, and for the benefit of the children there was a big oak tree at the back of the hall and church building. We were allowed to climb this tree, and I remember Buster once got stuck up it. I think someone had to climb up and fetch him down as he was too frightened to move. The headmaster was a Mr Stutt; he had two sons, Geoffrey and Martin. One was very much like him in appearance, and I remember I did not like one of them. I think they must have been about thirteen and fourteen. These are the only people I remember there by name.

Somehow I found myself in a foster home in Barnet, Herts. It was quite nice and I went to school. Running true to form, I played hookey. In case you do not know what this means, it is truant. I don't think I behaved very well as I used to upset Aunty May. I've a vague recollection she was pregnant, and therefore unable to cope with the very difficult child I had become. I think a lot of my disturbed state was due to the fact that Buster and I were separated. I had nothing at all I could call my own.

I was sent back to Harpenden and put on the hospital ward. At least I was seeing Buster again, but not for long. I cannot remember this myself, but during the writing of this book I have made inquiries concerning my past and the National Children's Home at Harpenden has been very helpful and filled a few gaps in for me.

From the information I was given I can tell you that I was sent next to Shrodelle Hospital at Watford for observation. This would be in 1943. From there I was sent to a workhouse in St Albans which is now the city hospital. I was then ten years of age and really cannot understand why I was there, and can get no further details from the respective authorities about *why* I was there, only the proof that I *was* there. This place was as I would imagine a prison to look – high walls, a big iron gate and a little lodge at the side. The wards were stark to say the least. They were painted cream and dark green with a dark brown line separating the two colours. The beds were black iron things with horrible lumpy mattresses, and I think the covers were red. The smell was dreadful.

The inmates were the oddest set of people I have ever seen.

They were old smelly women who wet their knickers and did the other in them too so they smelt to high heaven. They even talked to themselves and fought over the dreadful food. They carried little cloth bags with all their worldly belongings in them. Each able-bodied inmate had to work at some menial task, scrubbing floors, sweeping, the laundry work and all the dirty chores that had to be done in a place like that. I soon found a way to amuse myself. Perhaps I was unkind, but I thoroughly enjoyed myself. I used to tip the buckets over, throw their mops out through the window, pull blankets off beds, and run away with their little bags. I cannot remember any of the nurses individually. They all looked the same to me. Their uniforms were different from today's – the dresses were much longer and striped, and they wore stiff collars and cuffs, starched aprons, and the caps covered much more of the hair than today's do. They rustled as they walked.

The building had loads of wild cats living underneath it, and also in the pipes which ran down the side of the paths, and I too found a refuge with them. I pinched food and milk from the kitchens to feed the cats. They were always pleased to see me. I must have looked like the Pied Piper sometimes. At other times I helped the nurses with the old bed-ridden women. I learnt to rub their backsides, heels and elbows with methylated spirits, zinc and castor oil, finishing off with a rough powder. I learnt to roll them over to one side of the bed, enabling a soiled sheet to be changed, and even to feed some of them from feeding-cups with spouts.

I do remember the matron. She was not very old, had red hair, and a son of about my age. His name was Lewis Green. I did not like him very much. He used to sneak on me and tell his mother where my hideaways were. I wanted to belt him but dared not. Matron had made it quite clear to me that I would be punished by being locked in a small room for a week, so I was not risking that.

Here again memory eludes me, but from information given me I understand I was sent from this workhouse to a home called St Margaret's after being at St Albans for about six months. I cannot remember anything at all about St Margaret's, and the authorities are unable to give me the address. I can therefore only surmise that it was from here my mother came and took me out to her home in the little village of Westbury in Wiltshire.

2

Mother had a job as a district nurse at Westbury, and made it clear from the word go that she had a
position to uphold. Buster was home – I cannot remember if he
came before or after I did. It was a lovely little village and in
spite of all that was to come I remember that we were happy
there. We went to the Church of England school, which was
very old-fashioned compared with today's liberal views. The
headmaster was very severe. He always wore a gown and a
mortarboard, and always carried a cane or book in his hand.
We all called him 'Gaffer' Newman, but only when he could
not hear us. We had a very healthy respect for him. We had a
very nice music teacher. Her name was Miss Forsythe, and unlike
'Gaffer', she was very kind. She also taught English, a subject I
always did well at. The vicar was an extremely nice man, I
think his name was the Rev. Hinton. He was very understanding
and taught RI at school.

Buster and I were always skiving from school, and much to
Mother's dismay we found a wonderful orchard to scrump in –
but it was, of all people's, her landlady's, who was also one of her
nursing officers and sat on the local magistrates' bench. Mrs
Shoreland was her name, as far as I can recollect. I think it goes
without saying that we got caught and had one of the biggest
hidings I can remember. I don't think Buster or I sat without

wincing for days. We vowed we would not get caught again for we had no intention of not going back. They were lovely apples and worth the risk, plus the fact that we knew it annoyed Mrs Shoreland and Mother would get told off. Another prank was in the church. I used to push Buster into the little box at the side of the organ and get him to pump and I would play the organ with two fingers. That did not last long – the vicar caught us. I also got caught taking a big bow of ribbon from a wreath. It was so pretty I could not resist it. Fair play to the vicar, he really did try with us!

I think the next paragraph must be devoted to Scruffy. My mother said she got him from a bomb-site in London. He was a tiny little bundle that would fit in your pocket when she brought him home. Buster and I were delighted. I think Mother brought him for herself, but that was to be otherwise. Scruffy was a children's dog and followed us everywhere, even to school. We were always being told off by the headmaster as Scruffy used to wait in the playground for us. He grew into a huge animal with enormous feet. He used to creep upstairs to Buster's room, and it looked so funny to see Buster sleeping on the edge of the bed and Scruffy with the lion's share of the bed. When Mother caught him up there and hurled him out, he would come downstairs like a herd of elephants. To Buster, he was the most beautiful dog in the world. Disaster was to come to Scruffy. He and a dalmatian went chicken-stealing. The dalmatian got off with it, but poor Scruffy was shot. To this day Buster hasn't forgiven Mother for allowing it to happen. I think once more Mother was protecting her coveted position in the village – it didn't matter how Buster and I felt about losing our treasured friend. Mother immediately went out and got herself another dog. This was a wire-haired terrier bitch called Nipper, but she could never replace Scruffy.

Mother went into hospital to have a lump removed from her leg. When she came home she could not walk very well, so we borrowed an old lady's wheelchair and said we'd take her for a walk. Now, to understand the position completely, I must explain the layout of the houses where we lived. They were terraced, our terrace running along the top of a hill with two terraces of houses on either side of us. We started to wheel Mother down the hill, and just for the sheer buggery of it decided to let go of the wheelchair. I've never seen anything so funny – Mother trying to stop the wheelchair with her hands while screaming out to us to catch her. This was impossible, for by now the chair had gathered a good speed and Buster and I were laughing so much we couldn't do a thing. Fortunately for Mother a man near the bottom of the hill saw what was happening and came to the rescue. Mother was saved. Buster and I had seen no danger in it, and although the hill went straight on to a major road, we couldn't understand why everyone was so annoyed as we'd often come down this very hill in the same wheelchair. I cannot remember whether we got a hiding for that. I expect we did.

I think the village of Westbury where we lived is worth a mention. It was so pretty and had green hills for a background. Carved out on the hillside was a huge white horse, although I've never seen it white as at the time it was camouflaged by the army because of the war. I believe the horse was a mile if one walked around the complete outline. Buster and I used to take sandwiches and lemonade and spend the biggest part of the day up in the hills. We would sit on the horse's eye and eat our picnic. We would spend hours there. It always seemed like summer. I cannot remember any bad weather. Winter seemed only to come at Christmas. Another activity was swimming in the local baths.

After a while, Mother had an evacuee family, an RAMC sergeant, his wife and young son, John. Later, Aunty Alice, as we called her, had a little girl called Joy. She was born at home and I helped by bringing hot water upstairs to the bedroom. I can still see Aunty Alice's face twisted in pain. She was hanging on to a towel tied to the top of the bed. I was very surprised to see her a little later, safely delivered of Joy, looking so calm and peaceful.

Children can be very unkind to one another, and we were no exception. There was a poor girl in the village. She lived in the church cottages and the place was filthy. The child always had lice in her hair and was always badly dressed. We always ran behind her, shouting and jeering and calling her fleasy. How I regret this action now.

The village policeman lived only a few doors away from us, and although we liked and respected him, we had many a clip around the ear from Bobby Bevan. We ran like hell if he caught us up to mischief. It was all fair game. If you could run faster than the village bobby, you had won the day. His wife made wonderful pigeon and rook pies and often gave us one. They also had two evacuees – a nice girl called Wendy and a boy of about twelve or thirteen. He was horrible. He always had a runny nose. We used to call him Snotty.

I made a friend of a girl just down the hill, but Mother disapproved. Her mother was always out with the Americans. This did not bother me, as the Yanks, as we called them, were very good to us children. They threw candies, fruit, peanut-butter and coffee out of the lorries to us. I remember once taking Mother's bike and coming straight down the hill on to the main road. Here I tagged on to one of the American lorries, and I was hanging on to the back when the whole lot stopped suddenly. I came off the bike and the jeep following ran over the wheel of the bike. God help me! How on earth was I going to face Mother? I needn't have worried. The Americans took me home and said it was their fault and promised to buy Mother another bike. A new bicycle arrived for Mother the following morning with a big basket of provisions. I got out of that one nicely. We loved the Americans, cupboard-love though it may have been.

During my stay at Westbury I'd been in minor troubles with the law, but I can only remember the last and final time. Buster, myself and several other children got into the local food office through a small window that had been left open. We took orange juice and malt and even ate the dried milk. It was lovely! On the desk was a typewriter complete with paper. I just could not resist a go and left my name and Buster's blazened across the paper. That was it! I was up before the magistrates, and bless me if one of them wasn't Mrs Shoreland. I didn't stand a chance.

My mother said she could not cope with me and that I led Buster into trouble. All the reports were read out about me. The local bobby had his say, with the vicar and the headmaster of the school. The powers-that-be decided I must be sent away and recommended a remand home. The magistrates gave me a new title. They called me a 'problem child'. I liked this. At least I was something and people knew I was around. But I was now to taste the harsh discipline handed out to children who don't conform.

I was packed off to a remand home near Chelmsford in Essex. I think it was called Newport House. It was a big house with a drive and nice gardens to the side. As we went through the large doors, I was greeted by a very large masculine-looking woman dressed in a navy skirt and jacket. She wore her grey hair in an Eton crop. I immediately felt afraid of her. I was taken to a small room and my clothing was taken away. My hair was examined for nits, and then I was checked over by an elderly doctor and passed as fit. They gave me the school uniform, which was a white blouse, grey skirt and jersey, grey socks and black lace-up shoes, and a navy raincoat. This was everyday wear. Sunday best was printed dresses and white socks, straw hats and a blazer. The food was good and clean, and there were only a few girls in the home. But I did not like it one bit and hated the strict discipline, and even more Miss Asps, the headmistress. I started to draw away from people, going off alone to different parts of the garden or to the conservatory where I would sit for as long as they would let me, reading, doing a puzzle or, for some unknown reason, pulling the wings off flies. We had evenings when we had to darn socks. This I did not like, though I did not mind knitting. What I actually did to merit the punishments they gave me I cannot remember but I do clearly recall being on the receiving end of a cane, both on my hands and my backside.

There was also a detention room where I once spent many days. This was a small room with thick wire mesh over the window and just a mattress on the floor with a grey blanket.

To me this punishment was terrible. I shouted and screamed and tore at the wire on the window until my hands bled. Eventually someone gave me an injection to shut me up. This must have happened in one of the school holidays because two girls, who I was to meet again later, came to stay there as guests. I remember one was nicknamed 'Nosey Parker,' the other 'Tin Ribs'. Why they wanted to stay I don't understand. Every Sunday we went in a two-by-two crocodile across the fields to the church. Of course, everyone stared at us as they knew we were all from the remand home, but at least it got us out for a bit.

At the home we had to do jobs like sweeping and dusting and making the beds, and some of us had to help weed the head-mistress's garden. We did have a teacher there for schooling, but I wasn't very attentive. Several times I was taken before visiting boards. All the fuddy-duddies told me what a naughty child I was, but they might have saved their breath because by this time I did not care what anyone said. Just to be noticed was an achievement, and I'd done that all right. After some discussion it was decided to send me to an approved school in Liverpool. Now that did turn out to be a really tough place.

3

I arrived at the approved school, which was called St Christopher's and was at a small place called Great Crosby, just outside Liverpool. As usual, my first feeling was one of fear, and this time it was more justified than usual. I cannot remember my actual arrival, or the journey, but before leaving Chelmsford I do recall the headmistress of the remand home telling me I would have to behave myself in the place I was going to. I found it very hard, especially since punishment at St Christopher's seemed to be given for the slightest misdemeanour. One of the nastiest punishments was to have to scrub the outside yard with a sort of brick. This made your fingers bleed and caused chaps, which were very painful. We received no treatment for this. Perhaps it was part of the authorities' treatment for breaking our spirits, but it did not work on me.

Inside the building I can remember only three rooms. There was a large hall, with lockers that did not lock, a mess room and, of course, the unforgettable detention room which all these places seemed to have. As the lockers had no locks, it seemed to be a free-for-all. I remember losing my St Christopher's ring, also my precious kaleidoscope, and after even the most enterprising search neither of them was found. This upset me and because of the fuss I made I got the cane in front of the entire school, though on this occasion only on my hands.

We had singing. This I enjoyed and willingly learnt the yards and yards of the 'Walrus and the Carpenter', and for a change was not in trouble during recreation time. We also went to an outside school, but it did not last long for me as a girl and I ran away. We got into Liverpool, and to a place called Oriel Road, where the girl lived. To this day I recall the orange lights on the streets, and how it made out lips look mauve. We thought this very funny as I had never seen lights like them before. When we got to this girl's house (I cannot even recall her name or what she looked like) her mother gave us something to eat and drink and then, in spite of her daughter's pleading, called the police. After a very short time they arrived and we were taken to the police station. This was quite nice, and we were given more food and cocoa. I am sure the police were quite sympathetic towards us, but, of course, we had to go back. To what I was not sure, but we were soon to find out.

Back at St Christopher's we were taken before the whole school, and there we were stripped to our knickers and vests, then put across a chair, had our knickers pulled down and were caned across the backside. Needless to say, I kicked and screamed and was taken to the detention room. This tiny room had no furniture at all, only a mattress on the floor. The window was, as in the remand home, covered with a thick wire mesh, but had the added security of iron bars across the outside. I screamed for ages, but no one took any notice as this room was at the very end of the school, and no one really bothered how much noise you made. Because I played up I was put on a bread-and-water diet. This was only allowed for three days, and a doctor had to see you before and after the treatment. I cannot remember how long I stayed in detention.

By this time I had withdrawn completely from most things. I would not mix with the other girls, although there were one or two who were kind to me. I remember one called Edith, and little realized that I was to meet her again in stranger-than-ever surroundings. I can also bring to mind her little fag, fags being younger girls who, for protection and a liking for an older girl, would wait on her. Her fag would tell Edith if she heard anything. Some of the girls were really nasty and led the younger ones a hell of a life, even telling lies about them, which the staff seemed to believe.

I have tried very hard to recall some happier moments at this school, but for some reason I cannot. Memories of St Christopher's are almost obliterated, perhaps for the better. Maybe my mind, which at the time this happened was only eleven years old, was unable to cope with so much severity, so shut it out. I can only surmise, it is so long ago.

The next port of call was the Caldecott Community, at Hyde House, near Wareham in Dorset, and what a contrast to the approved school – who approves those places I would like to know?

A Miss Leila Randall ran Caldecott, along with a very able-bodied staff. These were people who really cared. You cannot fool a child, and one could feel they cared. I cannot recall any punishment. Of course, there must have been some form of discipline but it did not appear at all prominent and the welfare of the child came first. Do you remember I mentioned two girls who came for a holiday at the remand home at Chelmsford? Well, here I met them again. They were both without parents and had been living happily at Caldecott for a few years.

We were taught to ride here, and had three horses, the one for the learners being a lovely-tempered beast called Puff. She was broad as she was long, and when you sat astride her, your legs stuck out either side like yard-arms. We all loved Puff, and nothing was nicer than weekends when we took it in turns to ride her when we all went for walks. Muffin was another cup of tea and did not suffer fools gladly. He was an Arabian steed and was used in the local gymkhanas, and the girl who rode him was good. I envied her ability to take the jumps, and one day decided to have a go. It must have looked hilarious to any spectators! I got on Muffin all right and was full of confidence as we approached one of the small jumps. Then I lost my nerve, pulled the horse up, trying to veer away from the jump. It did not work. Over the hedge I went, but Muffin stayed behind. He had veered off at the last minute. I was not hurt, but I did get told off, as I could have hurt both myself and the horse. I never tried that again. The third horse was called Bramble. He was a big steed belonging to one of the teachers, and was a bony animal with enormous hooves. They told us he had had a disease of the hooves which caused this. Anyone who knows about horses who reads this will I am sure know what I mean. We were not allowed to ride Bramble as he was far too tall for us children. There were also two golden labrador dogs, whose names I cannot remember, but I do recall that the tiny grey kitten was called Misty and was a great favourite with the children.

Now, you must be thinking, I was surely settling down well by now. Alas, it was not to be. The care had come too late to undo all the previous neglect. I was still one of many, and the only way to be one alone was to be a darn pest, and even here it worked. I was not beaten, but, of course, they had to do something, as I still did not trust anyone, and not even the kindness of the staff could reach me. I used to wet my bed like some of the other girls who were there, and I would go with the others on a trip to the bathroom late at night. As always, I would be wet again in the morning, but the staff never chastised us for it.

One thing I did not like was being No. 18, which was my clothes-tag number. We were divided into different age groups. I was in the juniors, and I think, as in many other homes, girls and boys were separated. Although I can see faces, I remember very few names of the staff or other children. One of the older girls was very good to me. Her name was Dorothy and she tried to help where the staff could not, but suddenly she had gone. I was to meet her later in hospital.

Why I did not settle at Caldecott I do not know. It was a lovely place, with beautiful grounds, of which we received the full benefit. There were streams to paddle in, and fields to play in, and the mile-long drive was lined with rhododendrons. The food was nicely set out, and we had little pats of butter on our plates. At dinner time we all had a glass of cabbage water to drink. Some of the children hated this, but I liked it. The home was very clean. Some of the older girls used to help with the housework and we younger ones used to do the dusting sometimes, and help to clean out the stables. So what went wrong? Perhaps I was trying to establish an identity of my own. Who knows why one feels unable to conform?

4

After a lot of talk it was decided to send me to my first mental hospital. This was in London, and it happened over thirty years ago as I was then about eleven and a half years old. The hospital was like a big house, and was a very pleasant place. I was admitted on to what was called the admittance ward. The ward sister was young and very nice, and so were all the other nurses. I remember nothing else of this ward. I must have been difficult as I was moved on to a locked-up ward. It was on this ward that I began to get to know the medical superintendent and the matron who were to become the first people to get through to me. I did not behave for a long time, and it was in this hospital I had my first terrifying experience of a padded cell – a terrible form of treatment no longer used.

The padded cell was awful. It was cream-coloured rubber-padded stuff, and smelt horrid. There was a gutter around the edge and a light high in the ceiling covered with thick glass with wire in it. In the door was a round peephole, and on the floor a rubber mattress. The window was high and shuttered. The sense of complete isolation was dreadful: one felt almost smothered, and literally gasped for fresh air. While I was in this claustrophobic room my mother came to see me; I learnt she was working in a pharmaceutical factory in London.

I do not remember much of the visit, just that she came. A few days later I came out of the pads.

Pop, as I called the medical superintendent, was beginning to help me. He was a fatherly man of about fifty. Perhaps he was a substitute for the father I did not have. Pop had a bull-terrier dog called Bostock: he was a lovely dog, and when I was around he would go to no one else. He was as good as mine, and Pop did not mind. While I was on the locked ward, I developed osteomyelitis. This is an infection of the bone and mine was in the left tibia. I believe it can come up in an abscess, fortunately mine did not. I was given penicillin every three hours. It must have been winter time as my bed was next to the fire. I was very well cared for and was even allowed to have Bostock to see me. He was most annoyed because they would not allow him on the bed. Anyway, there was no room with the big cradle thing I had to keep the blankets off.

As with most healthy children, I healed well and was soon on my feet again. Bostock and I were by now inseparable. We had an old summer-house in the grounds, and I furnished it with anything I could lay my hands on – mats scrounged from Matron, books, pens, jigsaw puzzles, flower-pots, even old chairs. This was my little castle, mine and Bostock's. Even Pop always asked if he could come in. I had only one intruder. This was a mannish woman inmate who helped in the gardens. She had been there years, and had considered Pop and the dog her personal property, so was very peeved when I arrived on the scene. The day she came to my little domain was the first and last. I picked up everything I could lay my hands on and threw them at her, and when she tried to hit back Bostock flew at her. Poor Sybil, what with me and the dog snarling at her she cleared off, threatening all sorts of things. But I was not afraid of her. I had won my first battle against someone twice my size. It felt very good. Sybil never came near my little palace again, but I did get told off for tearing her jacket, and was told never to set the dog on anyone. Not that I'd told Bostock to join in. He'd thought I was being hurt.

By this time I was part of the family. Pop used to take me out with him, and we used to go to London Zoo, and to his bungalow, which was at Staines, on the River Thames. It was lovely. Matron used to come, or one of the sisters. I was so happy. I had the freedom of the hospital now, and came and went as I pleased. I used to get a penny platform ticket, and go up and down on the tube trains just for the fun of it. Pop was a very good photographer and developed his own films. It was fascinating to see the picture appear through the liquid. He took lots of photographs of Bostock and me together.

One day another girl came to the hospital, and I knew her from the approved school. Her name was Adele. I was pleased, for here was someone more my own age. Adele was sixteen and quite attractive. We got on very well, but Pop told me to be very careful. I did not understand what he meant, but was soon to find out.

One day Adele and I went out. We went to the railway sidings where there were some empty old carriages. It was here Adele met up with some young men. I did not quite realize what they were all up to, but sensed it was not quite right, so, after a very short while, decided to go back to the hospital. I told Pop, not meaning to tell tales but out of sheer ignorance. Adele was sent away from the hospital shortly after this incident. I heard later that she was pregnant, and I did know what that meant. It left me a bit lonely again, but Pop understood and I was encouraged to help with some of the treatment given to the other patients. Perhaps this was an unwise thing to do, but nevertheless it happened. I helped Pop with the electric treatment. There was always a nurse present, and we always asked the patient if they minded my being there. They never did.

The machine was a big thing about the size of a fridge or a washing machine. It had lots of knobs on it, and dials with wires coming from it. There was also a pair of things which looked like headphones, much larger than the ones we are used to seeing today. The patient was fully conscious and would be asked to remove any hair-grips, dentures and pins. Then she got on to a high bed, and her head was cleaned with a sort of spirit before some white stuff that Pop called contact lotion was put on the temples. I often did this for him. Then the machine was plugged into a big socket on the wall, the switches turned on, the headphones placed on the patient's head, a button pressed, and the patient knew no more for a little while. It was horrid to watch. They would go into a convulsion, and foam at the mouth, their limbs jerking. It reminded me of a dog I had once seen having a fit. I got used to seeing it, but I was still frightened by it.

By now I seemed to be a happy settled child, and would have been quite content to stay there for ever. I had been moved on to a 'villa' ward, as they always called the nicer wards, I don't know why. The villa wards were really luxurious, with thick pile carpets and lovely down eiderdowns, wash-basins in all the rooms and pretty curtains at the windows. I had never seen such a lot of good things in one place. Matron had a flat in the lower part of the villa. This was nice too, and I spent many happy hours there. Matron was engaged and her fiancé was a very pleasant young man. He was as kind to me as was Matron, and put up with my sauce good-humouredly. They often took me out with them.

The cook was very tolerant with me, too, especially as I was such a pest to her. I would want food at all odd hours for myself and Bostock. She'd tell me I was a bloody pest, but always with a smile on her face. I remember I once wanted some ice cream. Cook was busy and told me to help myself. I did. Bostock and I polished off nearly a week's supply between us. We were not even sick, but Cook tanned my backside, and when I told Pop he said it served me right. Well, it did really.

The world seemed to be my oyster. I used to go to the track to watch the greyhounds running. I found a plank loose in the fence and used to crawl through. This was fine until Bostock let me down. He started to bark at the greyhounds, so we got turned out, and they blocked my little hole in the fence up and that was that. We used to go swimming in the Thames at Staines. Pop had a little rowing-boat and Bostock and I would swim alongside. There was a little island opposite Pop's bungalow. I think it was Runnymede.

Unfortunately it was all soon to come to an end. As I was so well, there was no reason for them to keep me, so I was sent back to Caldecott. I learnt in later life that Bostock had to be destroyed as he fretted and turned nasty after I left. Poor Bostock, to die because he cared too much for me.

5

After the individualism, being one of many did not go down well with me. Also, I wanted to go back to Pop. I thought if I played up they would send me back to him, but it did not work that way. I cannot recall much of what happened on my return to Caldecott. I do remember Miss Leila used to try to talk to me, but she got nowhere. They had taken me away from the only place and the only people I had been happy with in my whole life, and I resented it and had no intention of making it easy for them. Eventually Caldecott sent me to another mental hospital, this time near Portsmouth. I was not frightened. As I had been so well cared for at Pop's hospital I did not expect any harshness. Now I still shudder at the memory of the place. It was terrible: the wards were large and bare, the grounds were surrounded by a high brick wall and there were no flowers.

Electric treatment was given here. There were rows of beds, and patients had to lie with their heads to the foot of the bed. Screens were moved between the beds as the treatment was given, and you could see and hear the ones the doctor had done. It was terrifying. I could see and hear all this, and was barely twelve years old. Then they decided to give me the treatment. I fought like a hell-cat, out of sheer fear. I would go under fighting and come round the same way, so what good it ever did me I don't know.

I thought it was used on me as a punishment, and I was petrified of the tubby doctor who gave the treatment. He was one of those people with a perpetual smile on his face, almost satanic to my terrified mind. I was put on a refractory ward, which is the name for a ward where there are violent patients. One nurse on this ward was really cruel. She would pull my hair, twist my arms up my back, and punch me. She was very careful never to mark me, but who would have noticed if she had? It was no use complaining. The smiling doctor would just keep on smiling at me as though I were an idiot. He was most unnerving; I was so terrified of the ECT. I used to sit in the corner, watching the clock and waiting for them to come and get me. I really cannot describe the terror I felt for this man and his machine. I can still feel those very feelings now thirty years later, and find it difficult to write about this passage of my life coherently. I am sure the ECT caused the many blanks in my life and it has certainly obliterated many childhood memories.

It was at this hospital that I met Dorothy from Caldecott again. She had been here for quite a while. I could not talk to her much, as she was on a different ward. At one time I was put on to a villa ward, which was not too bad, in fact a great improvement on the locked wards. There was a big cellar under the house, and it was nearly always flooded. Living down there were lots of lizards, newts and frogs. I used to go down with another girl and catch them. Often their tails used to come off in my hands and they would get away. The sister on the ward was very nice – a change from the one on the lock-up ward. A girl on the villa whom I got friendly with was called Angela, I think. She was older than me, and very nice. We got on well together.

Why I was taken from this ward and put back on a locked ward I cannot recall. I now found myself on a ward for old women. In charge of this ward was a very nice Irish sister, who was kindness itself to me. The ward was horrible: it had no mats, only scrubbed floors, as the old women used to wet and mess themselves. Many were bedridden, and only there because their relatives could not be bothered with them. Here, as at the

26

St Albans workhouse, I helped with the old ladies by washing and greasing their backsides. I must have been thirteen now, and was starting to develop as young girls do. They were still giving me ECT and I was still as terrified of it. I remember coming round from the ECT, and Sister with several other nurses was trying to pour paraldehyde down my throat. It was an evil-smelling drug, and tasted foul. It burnt your throat as it went down, and is a taste you can never forget.

I recall that I did see a lady doctor – she was a child psychiatrist, whatever they are. She asked me lots of questions about my past and my mother. I cannot remember my replies, but I do remember making little figures with plasticine. I always made a model of Mary and Jesus – perhaps, to my mind, this depicted a happy mother-and-child relationship, the one I had been deprived of. It's only a guess, but one seems to expect a reason for one's actions. I cannot bring many other people into my story, for although it may seem that I am wrapped up in myself, the reason is simply a lack of recall. The things remembered seem to be the unhappiest thoughts, and try as I may I can find very little joy in this part of my life.

I do recall the first boy who took an interest in me. He was at the hospital, too. He was about sixteen, and his name was Derek. He used to bring me sweets, and books, and if we could we would walk around the grounds together. I was to meet Derek again, but not under happy circumstances.

While I was on the old women's ward my mother came – and was allowed to take me out for two weeks' holiday. She was living at Weston-super-Mare in Somerset. Here she was once again the district nurse. She had a nice furnished house and I had a very nice holiday. She took me to see all her cronies and the time went quickly. Buster was by now in the Duke of York's Royal Military Academy, where Mother had sent him after I was sent to the remand home, and was not home yet. The holiday passed, and Mother returned me to the hospital. I had only been back on the ward about half an hour before a nurse from the office came for me. She told me I was going home for good. Mother had decided she wanted me back, and against medical advice had signed me out.

We went back to Weston and a few days later Buster came home. He was quite tall now – I had not seen him for about four and a half years. It was nice to see him. Next came the inevitable lecture from Mother: to think of her position as the nurse, and to remember that this house was rented, so be careful. It seemed the same old song; Mother had not changed.

We had a row one morning, and after a slap around the face from her I ran from the house. Where I was going I didn't know; all I wanted was distance between her and myself. Mother called in the aid of a passing man, who gave chase. They cornered me in an alley. I tried to shin up the wall, and I don't know whether it was in my fevered imagination that I thought I heard Mother saying to the man, 'Knock her out, please knock her out!' He didn't anyway – by strange coincidence he was a Red Cross man. They took me home, and after lectures and threats from Mother, the incident passed. By this time Buster was back at military school, and I was alone in the house, and other than the child next door, saw no one. I'd take this child to the park and play in the garden with him. Each week Mother took me to a probation officer, who was a nice understanding lady, but with Mother always in the room I could tell the lady nothing of how I felt. I just had to listen to Mother saying what a problem I was.

By now I was nursing real hatred for this woman who had given me life, or was it life? I hoped each day that perhaps she'd go away for ever, and at the same time I'd feel deep guilt for feeling like this. I knew she was my mother, but other children's mothers loved them and showed that they did. If we fell over, we had to pick ourselves up. There was no 'Kiss it better', only a bottle of iodine and, 'You'll die after it.' You never cried; that was a sign of weakness. How you love someone who seems to find it impossible to love back I do not know. You can't, I'm sure, so guilt is a pointless agony. Buster didn't seem to mind as much as I did, but later I knew it had its effect when I saw how very hard he had grown in some of his attitudes.

I took the dominance of Mother as long as I could. Then one

day, with nowhere to turn and feeling I'd rather die than stand any more, I took the final step which was to lead me further away from normality and the hope of a loving home which was really all I wanted. I took an overdose of barbiturates. I didn't count them: I wasn't crying for help, I wanted out, so I took all there were. Fortunately (those were not my feelings then) I lived, but in those days a suicide attempt had to be reported to the police, and I was sent on an order to my third mental hospital in three years.

I came to this rather isolated mental hospital at the end of the summer. It lacked all the comforts found in our modern hospitals, having no carpets or easy chairs, very few flowers or plants, walls of green and cream paintwork, and bare wooden floors. The windows were high and small so there was no view of outside. The rooms were small and grim with heavy doors that had slits in for the peephole. It was into one of these rooms that I was put. As usual a doctor came and gave the usual physical check-up. Then the most awful-looking food I can remember was given to me. The potatoes were so full of eyes they almost winked, the cabbage almost walked off the plate, and the greasy gruel called mince – ugh! The porridge bears mention too, it was a solid gooey grey mass, and tasted as bad. Why I didn't die of malnutrition, I don't know. I suppose I got used to it.

After a few days of non-cooperation with the staff and doctors, I was put on the closed ward. What a place! Some of the difficult patients were locked in the bottom of the ward, and to my horror I found they'd fight for the food off your plate, screaming and pulling your hair. Here was another problem I'd got to cope with if I wanted to exist.

The staff nurse on this ward was really nice, and in the time spent here I experienced no cruelty, even when I was difficult. I learnt to open the dividing door between the top and bottom parts of the ward with a knife. I could only do this at meal times since the cutlery was always counted and put away, and on the lower ward they had only spoons. There was one woman in her thirties on the ward. She'd had a baby son, and shortly after the birth had had milk fever. I don't know if this was what had made her mentally ill, but that's what I was given to understand. I'll call her 'Milly', for when she was all right she became a good friend to me, and woe to anyone who touched me. Not that I needed any protection, for by now I was totally anti-social and fully equipped to cope with any hand raised against me, even striking first if I thought it was to my advantage.

Milly and I were always together and she shared her food parcels with me, and when I had anything I gave her some. When they locked me in for misbehaviour, in too went Milly. She treated me as her own child. I remember what it was like being locked in. The windows of the rooms were covered by heavy wooden shutters, and it was difficult to climb up, as the window sills were deeply slanted. Very heavily drugged, I would get out of the bedding on to the floor, and for the life of me would not be able to find the bedding again. I could see a light through the slit in the door, and would try to stand up but was too heavily sedated; so to draw attention to my plight I would lie on my back and kick the door with my feet. Eventually the nurse would come, only to give me another injection. This, I understood, was known as insulin sleep treatment.

I do stress that in spite of many drugs given me here, to the extent that I was almost physically weak, I knew at all times what I was doing, stupid and very often detrimental to me as my actions may have been. Most of my time in this hospital I spent locked in my room, and I'd not disagree with a report I saw written about me: 'This patient is aggressive and abusive, very uncooperative, sedation given . . .' and quoting the dosage and 'remaining patients appear as usual'. This last phrase meant that I was the only disruptive one that day.

I was very amused when I read this a few days later, as I'd no intention of being a good girl. My aim now was to be as big a nuisance as possible, and I was doing very well by my thinking. I managed to shock one of the Irish nurses. She locked me on the wrong side of the door, so I kicked in the panel and crawled through. This wasn't what appalled her, it was my four-letter word when I tried to get away from her. That nurse never spoke to me again, and believe me, I tried to make her. I wonder how she copes with today's language.

Mother visited me with Buster, and she brought the dogs. I enjoyed that. Another time she came alone, and had a big baby doll for me. This started me off on knitting, a hobby I find very useful now that I have six children of my own to clothe.

While the patients on the ward were pretty far gone, and some were quite violent, my behaviour matched theirs. I swore and fought as good as the worst of them. There were times when I got fed up with playing up, and these times were rewarded by trips to occupational therapy and the hairdresser's. I did not display any special gifts at occupational therapy as I only found out I had any such gifts much later on. I can't really remember doing anything else other than play with the cats, which were semi-wild and often bit me when I tried to hold them.

The ward had an exercise yard, very much like what one sees on television programmes of prison yards, with high brick walls around. They had no flowers or shrubs, unlike present-day hospitals. I used to climb up the wall, and after they managed to get me down with the help of male nurses, I'd be put back in my room. My conduct was as I desired: deplorable, and in spite of the kindness shown me by an elderly Irish doctor and the staff nurse, I continued on a downward track.

On one of my 'good' days I recall seeing a lot of people around, and some of the cleaners very red-eyed. I was told later that a seventeen-year-old cleaner had been found dead in her room. She'd had peritonitis. She was a nice little Welsh girl, and like many others I was very sorry that she'd died.

On my sixteenth birthday, or around that time, I went before a doctor. My mother was present at the interview. He asked me questions that I viewed with contempt. Just how stupid did he think I was? He asked me the difference between an orange and a lemon, and was pretty annoyed when I told him to 'suck it and see'. Well, I ask you, any fool should know that. Then ink-blobs on blotting paper, round pegs in square holes. I felt it was the doctor who needed his head looking at. My obvious aggression towards him sealed my fate, and Mother signed a form. I was told I was going to a school for corrective training where I'd be taught useful things and made to behave. My God, if only they'd known what they were doing to me. I look at my own children now, and as their ages range from sixteen to four years, I think of where I was at their respective times of life – perhaps envying them a little, the home they have, the security, and best of all, in spite of them getting a wallop now and then, the love they have from their parents. It has made me realize how young a child can be, even at sixteen years.

The 14 November 1948 is a day I remember. It was Prince Charles's birthday and the day I was sent to Rampton.

6

The staff nurse and one other were the 'escort duty', and we travelled in a big black saloon car. I was given sweets and sandwiches and thoroughly enjoyed the ride. We passed through Coventry and they slowed down to let me see 'Lady Godiva'; I bet she was cold. We arrived at Rampton in the early afternoon. From the outside, unless you know where to look, you can't see an awful lot. Other than the two nurses' residences on each side of the road and in front of the entrance doors, there is a round sort of island with roses and shrubs. The building looked very large and awesome to me, and as we walked up the large steps, I wanted to run, but was unable to do so, being firmly held each side by the mental-hospital nurses.

We finally got through the doors and were greeted by a man in uniform who I learnt later was a 'screw'. I was duly signed in and handed over to one of the state nurses. I was taken through reception and down a long low-ceilinged corridor, and to my horror noticed big thick bars on the windows. It seemed just like a prison. Dear heaven, what were they going to do with me? We continued down the corridor, passing through two locked doors, which the nurse opened with a large key on a big thick chain – a thing I was to see a lot more of.

Next stop was a tiny office, in which was the sister on duty. She was a big woman with red hair, and she bore a striking resemblance to Greer Garson, so I'll call her Sister Greer. (The staff nurses were usually married and we always referred to them as Mrs So-and-So, using their surnames.) In this tiny office I was stripped naked, measured and checked for hair and body lice. While all this was going on, I was aware of people peering at me through the peephole, and Sister Greer giving a roar at them to clear off.

After lots of questions and being stripped of any identity I might have had, I was dressed in a shapeless gown and put in a cell. By now I felt scared half to death. The cell contained an iron bed and a locker plus a tin jerry. The barred window was heavily shuttered with a metal door-like piece, and the sill slanted so you could not look out of the small grill at the top. The door was metal, with two spy-holes in it, one at the top and one at the left bottom so that the staff could see into the corner of the room. There were also large brass ventilators at the bottom of the door, the inside of which was lined with some sort of metal sheeting.

Feeling very tearful and frightened, I wept. It was while I was crying I met the first inmate. She was an elderly woman, overweight and not very well featured, and this was Beaty. She told me to cheer up, asked my age, where I'd come from and what I'd done. The latter question I couldn't answer, as although I'd been a bloody pest, I'd done nothing criminal. The next thing I heard was a lot of people coming up the corridor, and many paused to say 'Hello love' as they passed my door on their way to the mess room for tea. My tea was brought in by a girl I later knew as Winnie. She was only nineteen. The food wasn't good, though it was a slight improvement on that in the previous mental home. The plate was tin, and on it was a greyish gooey mixture called fish pie, complete with bones. Also with it were two half-rounds of bread, and in a tin cup a drink which could have been tea, coffee or cocoa, but at least it was hot and wet.

After a while a doctor came to see me. Dr Terry was a big and pleasant woman, with glasses. Kind, but no fool. She didn't waste words. I liked her instantly and was sure I'd always be treated fairly by her. A day or so later I was taken to the bath-room. This was my first look around, and I noted that there were fifteen cells on the corridor. It was called by everyone 'the fifteen'. Near the end was a washroom, and round the corner the bathroom. I was surprised to see the taps: they had no tops on, and the nurse who was with me put a thing called a bath key on them and out came the water. I don't think this nurse liked me any more than I did her. Mrs Meadows was the type who really, as we said, 'took it out' on those she didn't like. After all, these nursing warders were human, and doing a diffi-cult job at times, and one must understand the different reasons they had for doing a job like that. Some, without question, were sadists; others enjoyed the feeling of power over their fellow humans; while many simply thought it a worthwhile job. To us, the inmates, they were either good or bad.

The next thing to be done was to fit me out with clothes. I was taken out of the ward and along to the sewing room. There I was measured by the lanky, fair-haired and rather impatient sister in charge of the sewing room. This was Sister Long. I was then taken back to the ward. The following morn-ing I asked if I could have my shutter open and Dr Terry said yes.

By this time I was beginning to know a few of the 'girls', as we called each other regardless of age. There were two other new girls with me – Pat and Joyce, who were both older than me. Joyce was rather backward, but a pleasant enough girl. I went around for a while with Winnie, but this didn't last long as her companion in 'her corner' was an aloof piece, and well in with the staff, so one had to be careful what one said, and so I moved. Each day, girls were sent to different places to work: to the laundry, sewing room or occupational therapy. I was put in the sewing room. What a disaster. I hated sewing. We had to herring-bone the edges of bed-jackets and nighties. My poor fingers! We'd start work at nine o'clock, at 10.30 there was a drink, and at twelve o'clock, back to the ward for dinner.

I'd not been in Rampton long before I saw the first of many forms of frustration that could build up among the girls.

35

Winnie suddenly smashed lots of windows, there was blood all over the place, and the staff appeared from nowhere. Winnie was taken to a place called the isolation in a separate building that I was to see sooner than I expected. Days in Rampton, which I learnt had once been a criminal lunatic asylum, passed slowly. The matron or her deputy came round every morning. I really disliked Matron, a woman with marmalade-coloured eyes. The rest of the daily routine was as follows: breakfast at eight o'clock, work from nine o'clock to midday; dinner at 12.15, then a time from 12.25 to 2 p.m. when you went to the recreation room to read, talk, knit, do jigsaws or dance to the radio. Two o'clock to four o'clock was work again; tea was at 4.30, and at 7 p.m. you were locked in your cells. That's just a brief outline.

The girls, myself included, were all certified as mentally deficient, and we were a mixed bunch – homosexuals, murderers, girls detained at HM pleasure, girls who had done little more than have sex too often, resulting perhaps in illegitimate babies, and a few of the girls had VD. There were the young girls who had been reared in institutions and landed up at Rampton. (The mothers of two of these girls had been here in the past.) There were some very violent girls, of whom even the staff were cautious, and there were really poor things who were certainly mentally retarded and had even their features and bodies distorted. We called these unfortunates 'wops'. There were quite a lot of epileptics as well. Some were terrible to see in their fits, but other than loosening their clothing and, once the fit was over, turning them on their sides, one could do little for them.

Unlike what I've read about prison life, the girls in Rampton showed no loyalty to one another. You couldn't plan to run off. Someone would always tell the staff. If you managed to smoke you could guarantee someone would split on you, and to be caught smoking was punishable by a spell on the isolation block.

I had been working in the sewing room for about two months until one day I was told off for some petty thing. In reply I stuck my tongue out at a nurse. Was I in for a shock! She lost her temper, jumped up and came round the table at me like a mad thing. Then the other staff joined in. I was by this time fighting and hanging on to the table. My hair was pulled and I was punched in the stomach and finally overpowered. With my arms up my back and Sister Long pulling my hair, I was dragged to the isolation block. This was a terrible place, and as the name suggests was completely isolated from all the other wards. Once inside, the staff in charge of the ward joined in hitting me and I was throttled unconscious for the first time. This is a nasty thing to experience, to say the least. Your tongue feels as though it's twice the size, your eyes feel as though they are going to pop out, and your ears feel ready to burst. Going unconscious is almost a relief. I was terrified. Throttling was usually done with a bath towel twisted round the neck, as this leaves no mark. After this I recall one of the staff saying, 'Come on, come on, wake up, Noele, are you all right?' My throat was sore and in my fright I thought, my God, they could kill you here, and no one would know or care.

The cell I was put in was awful, the corner of the floor covered in sediment from the continual urinating of a permanent patient. The ceiling had a fan in it, which was on continuously and made a monotonous whirring noise. The windows had two shutters over them, and there were two doors to the cell, the inner one being metal, the outer one wood. The bedding consisted of two ticking rugs which were hard and stiff as they were made of the material used to cover mattresses, several layers machined criss-cross together, but I had no mattress. The floor was damp, recently scrubbed, and I was kept in this room all day every day and only moved to another when this one was scrubbed. Our meals were thrown in on tin plates, with only a spoon to eat with, and in with the food would come a dirty smelly black rubber pot, which we had to use as we were not allowed out to the toilet.

It was on this ward that I met Violet. Gosh, was she ugly! But she had the most beautiful feet I'd ever seen, though when she was out on the exercise yard her hands would be tied in a shawl, or sometimes she was put in a strait-jacket. Her hands were tied because if she got her hands into your hair, no matter how hard you hit her she'd hang on kicking. Her feet were bare whatever the weather, as she had a kick like a mule. She also spat, and rarely missed her target. Everyone knew Violet. She was nicknamed 'Nicky'. People kept their distance. One morning Matron was doing her rounds and she opened the spyhole to say good morning to Nicky, and Nicky spat straight in her eye. I thought this was funny. The staff always had to go in twos to Nicky, as she'd go for them as well. There were two other regulars on the ward. Why they were there I don't know. I never saw them do anything violent.

How long I was on isolation ward I can't remember, but I didn't like it one bit. Eventually I went back to my own ward, and after a while regained the privileges I'd lost when going on the isolation. There were pictures on a Tuesday evening and a dance on a Thursday. Both recreations were held in the big hall. The dances were useful as it was at these we girls were able to get cigarettes from our boyfriends. It had to be done very carefully with the help of two friends who had to cover you from the staff and the other girls who might split on you. Also the men had to push the cigarettes into the front of our dresses. The punishment, if you were caught, was a spell on the isolation block. I was lucky, I never got caught, so it was worth the risk, as cigarettes were a valuable trading commodity. Some of the girls would give anything away for them. Another perk from the men were cigarette ends. These were in great demand for making snuff. The girls would get all the tobacco out of the butts, and then dry it out by putting it in paper and tying it round a radiator. When it was dry, they'd rub it, or roll it, until it was like powder, and ordinary washing soda would be added. This was then complete and was kept in little tins. Many of the girls were really dependent on the stuff and even used to sell their monthly sweet ration to the staff to get them to save their cigarette ends for them. The sweet ration was paid for by the girls out of the pittance they earned, usually a few shillings a month. A lot of girls did knitting for the staff, crocheting and embroidery. This work was beautifully done and the girls were grossly exploited, as the payment for these skilfully done jobs was very often only a bar of soap or a few cigarette ends, or some little thing which the girl needed that we couldn't get inside and so was considered a luxury.

After a while I was put on to another ward. Why they were called wards I don't know, as anything less like a hospital I've yet to come across. This ward was called B3, and the sister in charge was called Sweetman. I liked her, but a lot of the girls didn't. She was very strict, but I never once saw her ill-treat a girl. One of the things the girls did not like was folding up their beds every morning. We also had to scrub our rooms before breakfast. Of course, each night before you could get into bed, you had to make it. This was not very nice in the winter, but still, it became a habit, and we did it without thinking eventually. Sister Sweetman also had a very high standard of cleanliness, and her ward really was the cleanest and shiniest in the whole institution. I found that she never asked me to do anything she would not do herself. I have even seen her scrubbing the patients' toilets and polishing the walls. I know it sounds daft, but we really did have to polish the walls with Min polish. We also had loads of brasses to clean. These were on the walls, and there were also windows to clean. I certainly learnt how to do domestic work on this ward, and I can say I am pleased I did, as it has stood me in good stead.

Some of the girls were what we called 'big girls'. These girls you had to be cautious of. They seemed to have the run of this ward, and it was stupid to try and cross them. Maybe they were lifers, or maybe the staff were scared of them. I don't know, but I soon learnt to keep out of their way as much as possible.

Being young, I came in for my share of ridicule. The older girls told of their sexual experiences, and as I had none to relate I was called a liar. I was finding it very hard to get accepted by some of these tough girls. The language was terrible, and at first I did not swear, but after being called 'Lady Shit' a few times, I soon became as good, or shall I say as bad, as the rest. The use of swear words became everyday vocabulary: 'fucking this and that', or 'bollocks', and all the other usual ones, plus

39

songs that were screamed at the top of your voice when you were put in your room, or in seclusion, as it was called. One of them went like this (to the tune of 'Dinah'):

Way down in old Rampton, where bullshit is thick,
Where bum-boys are plenty, and babies come quick,
There sweet Carolina, the girl I adore,
She's a fucking old bastard, and bloody old whore.
She's dirty, she's poxy, and fucks in the street,
Whenever you see her she's always on heat.
If your flyholes are open, she'll grab at your meat,
And the smell of her cunt knocks you clean off your feet.

Another went thus (to the tune of 'Macnamara's Band'):

She's mad, she's mad,
A little bit off her top.
They gave her a bottle of paraldehyde,
She thought it was whisky pop.
The doctor he examined her,
Said, 'Water on the brain.
She's mad, she's mad,
She will never be right again.'

When it came to cursing, I found I was beginning to be one of the girls. I still had to progress to cutting my arms as yet, and this hurt, so at first you had to practise. I could only do little scratches and never really got into the big league of self-inflictions, as it is called. But my initiation to the life I was expected to lead had begun. I didn't really mind, as I wanted to belong to something. I couldn't have stood the jeers of the girls if I had not behaved in this detrimental fashion.

The girls always talked of their past, never the future, because unlike convicted prisoners we had no set time to do. We were there for ever as far as we knew. Some girls had been there over twenty years, so it was pointless to discuss the time when you would be free. I always said I'd write about what had happened in Rampton, but always got laughed at. But even then I was determined to make some sort of gesture to let the world know outside what went on behind those walls.

We used to plan to run away. Pat and myself plotted to hop it. We were going to take off when they took us to a sort of school they had for us younger girls. We were sitting in a corner with another girl called May who'd been there years, and rumour had it she once killed someone. I was quite prepared to believe it as she was capable of anything and even the staff were cautious of her. Pat and I were speaking in what we called back slang, done by putting the first letter of a word to the back and adding 'ay'; for instance, 'home' becomes 'omehay'. We were using this method to plan our escape, not knowing May understood. She went and told Mrs Meadows. As Mrs Meadows disliked me to start with, things looked pretty black for Pat and me. To get hold of something like this was really a thing this nurse would like. As May had split on Pat and me, we were watched and stopped from going to the classes. This seemed to upset Pat more than it did me, and that night in the dormitory Pat smashed some windows. She was taken to the isolation block and I had a hell of a life for several days. Mrs Meadows tried all ways to make me do something stupid. She stopped my privileges, saying I'd sworn at her. It was untrue, but what could I do? Even the girls were against me and I was called yellow. It took ages to cool down.

I got through this nasty phase, and began mixing with a new girl called Lydia. She was a worldly girl, and the mother of two beautiful boys. Lydia had letters and photographs regularly from her sons – I think she was about twenty-three. She was not in any way violent, but could she romance! She had also been in Holloway women's prison, and her tales of prison life were amazing, to say the least, and her experiences with men were unbelievable.

To understand the next item, I will have to explain why such extraordinary lengths were necessary. When we girls had a period, we were only allowed eight sanitary towels, so Lydia taught me how to make a tampon as this made the towels go further. We used to cut a towel into four bits, then wound white cotton round them. This was very useful. Lydia also told us about lesbians (we were that green!). She even said she was one, but we never believed her as she had her two sons.

Several girls had paired off as married couples. Pat had her girl, as they called them, and there was some form of sexual relationship between them. At this time I was not very interested in this aspect of life. I was too busy trying to adjust to the completely alien way of living I had found myself in. Also I was trying to come to terms with an authority which I both resented and hated. I hated being locked up, hated the awful clanking of great big keys every time a door was opened. Until you lose your freedom and are physically detained against your will, it's hard to realize how precious liberty is.

I heard pretty regularly from my mother and everyone said how lucky I was to have such a good mother. If only they knew what had really gone on, but they did not, so what was the use of trying to explain to girls who had no one? To them anyone who wrote a letter was good. I did feel sorry for those girls who had no one to give them outside chat.

There were times when I was easily upset; these times seemed to be prior to a period, and almost every time I was in trouble, regardless of form, it was always before the menstrual period. I would have thought this fact would have been noticed, but I was never given any help at these times, only punished. In all my eight years and a half in Rampton, I was given no medication to help any problem I may have had. The only drug I was given was the dope called paraldehyde and some form of antibiotic when I had a bad throat.

After a while I was put to work in the occupational therapy – OT as I will refer to it from now on, since that was what we called it. This I really enjoyed. I must be artistically inclined, for I soon found my way in clay modelling. This I was very good at, and I could express myself in my work. I could depict some of the violence I saw on the wards and also my hatred of certain things. It was a marvellous outlet. I progressed and was able to do portrait modelling and get a very good likeness. I was considered good enough to do a bust of the medical superintendent. This I enjoyed as I had an opportunity of speaking to him. Dr McKay was a good man, and throughout my time in this place I found him to be understanding, and very helpful. He was an interesting man, and asked me a lot of questions, but always very cleverly avoided answering any of mine. I'd ask why I was there, and he would reply with a question, asking me why I thought I was there. I'd ask when I would be going away, and again he would evade the query by asking where I would like to go. He would ask me about my mother, and this was a subject I could not easily answer, as I had this awful feeling of guilt for not loving her, so, apart from telling him that she was a nurse, I closed up. I found these sessions with the superintendent very helpful. I did not have to pretend. He knew how I felt by my conversation, and said if I had a problem I was to get in touch with him. Sometimes this was easier said than done, as one had to write for an appointment, and sometimes, I am sure, such letters were not forwarded to him. They had to go to the general office first, and if there was a complaint in them I'm sure they were withheld.

The OT was run by an elderly Scotswoman called Mrs Calvin. She wasn't too bad, but could be pretty unkind when she wanted to be, and at times I found her totally unreasonable. This was very frustrating, but just one other thing I had to contend with, as at other times she could be very helpful. I think she had a lot on her own plate, as she cared for an invalid mother and so, like the rest of us, had her off-days. The work done in the OT department was really good. Other than modelling, I learnt to do very fine embroidery, weaving, toy-making, rug-making. We also made stools and lampshades, and some of the girls made children's clothes. I was not a very good plain sewer – it was something I did not enjoy. But if there was a design or picture involved, I liked that. Tapestry was a great pleasure. Some of the girls made lovely Nottingham lace. It was quite a skilled task, and a thing I never really mastered.

I was usually happy in the OT room because, doing modelling, I was left alone as they could not do much to help me and there were no other girls who did it like I did. There was a pottery wheel, and some of the girls were very good on it and made some lovely pots, but while I could do the pottery, my preference was modelling.

At weekends we stayed on the wards and helped with the domestic chores. We had big bumpers, and you swung these to and fro to get a good shine on the floor. The second in charge to Sister Sweetman, Ma Sikes, was not as nice, though the third, a Mrs Cox, was not too bad, and left you alone. Not so Ma Sikes. If she'd got it in for you, she would make you work all day. Some of the girls liked her, but I did not – I cannot really say why, as she never hurt me. I think the person I disliked most on the ward was a big cock-eyed patient called Lottie, and I made no secret of it, though I tried to keep out of her way. There was also a girl called Joan, who did the most exquisite crochet work I've ever seen. She could do anything, from almost gossamer-like things to heavy shawls. She was a very pleasant, quiet person and I often sat with her as she never got into any trouble.

All the cleaning was done by hand. We had no hoovers, and had to sweep all the rooms out and the stairs down. After sweeping, the stairs had to be scrubbed and the floors polished, so cleaning took up quite a lot of our time.

I think it bears a mention that many of the staff who looked after us – or rather who kept us locked in – were sworn to some form of secrecy. Apart from that, many of them were not trained nurses. They had been there since the time dot, and had worked their way through the ranks, just by long service. Whether it is same today I do not know, but this I do feel: there should be new blood introduced, and jobs should not be handed down from mother to daughter like they were when I was there. I also think that it is stupid bureaucracy to have any form of secrecy applied in the case of the mentally ill or the mentally deficient (as I was called). This sort of secrecy breeds violence. I may add that, in 1957, before I left, some of the staff were beginning to go away on courses, and a few came back with their SRNs, but these were far too few. Of course, I must bear in mind while writing this book that I am referring to events twenty years ago.

To get back to the everyday things on the ward, in spite of

the rigid discipline, I was not getting on too badly at this time. Lydia was with me, so was Pat, and several other girls I'd been with on the admitting ward, so we were all about the same in terms of the time we'd been there. Again I started to knit and I made my mother a jumper. This I did in a rib and pattern, and it looked quite smart. Then I thought I'd add a nice personal touch to it, and embroidered 'MOTHER' across the front. I was very pleased with the result, and was looking forward to a visit from Mother so as to give it to her. Finally the great day came. I proudly handed the jumper to Mother, and at the same time put my arms round her. As usual, her remark was, 'Don't be silly child, control yourself'; then came the final dampener. To my eyes the jumper was beautiful, and I was very disappointed that Mother did not enthuse over it. I can see now you do not go around with 'MOTHER' blazened across your chest, but I am sure that if a child of mine had put so much care into something I'd have pretended. It's not as though I would have ever seen it on – but still, I suppose I'm wiser through these experiences. Thinking about my disappointment over this particular visit, I recall my elder daughter sending me a birthday card. On it was '41 today'. I suppose it's the same sort of thing that I did to my mother. I may add my reaction to this was one of laughter. I thought it was a lovely gesture. But Mother could not cope with that sort of demonstration, so I can understand and even feel sorry for her as being loved by anyone is a wonderful thing. This I know, having been without love for the biggest part of my childhood.

To get to the visiting room, visitors had to come down the long low corridor I'd first seen when I arrived. It must have been strange to them to have the doors locked after them and to see the bars on the windows. After each visit we were searched before returning to the ward. Back on the ward, I shared the sweets and cakes Mother had brought me with my particular friends, and got back into the humdrum routine. Oh, I almost forgot, Mother had brought me in some new red shoes, as we were not allowed to wear our own.

We had a girl called Christine on the ward. She was very pretty with fair curly hair and a nice trim little figure. She was very quiet, and quite popular. Why she made such terrible self-inflictions on her arms I don't know. In all my life I have never seen such gashes. They went from the top of her arm down to the elbow, and were very deep, always requiring lots of stitches. Her arms looked terrible. It seemed such a pity, as she never hurt anyone. Another girl used to swallow knives and was rushed to Sheffield Hospital several times. We called her the ostrich. She was quite a clever girl, and must have felt very desperate to go to such lengths. No one seemed to care very much, and they ignored the obvious cry for help from this girl.

I was still quite green in many ways, and having got myself all dolled up for a dance – and maybe as teenagers do even to this day, I had probably overdone things a bit, or maybe a lot – I was very upset when Mrs Cox told me I looked like a third-rate prostitute. It completely spoilt my evening, and although it may seem a minor thing, I brooded on it and the next time the doctor was sitting for a modelling session told him. After I went back to the ward Mrs Cox was sent for and the doctor reprimanded her. She was very quiet with me after that, but did not do anything to make life difficult for me, although Ma Sikes was quite nasty and told me to be careful how I trod. Believe me, for a while I was.

At about this time there was a craze going around for pierced ears, and I wanted mine done. A girl used to do them by pushing a darning needle through the ear. Surprisingly it was not too painful, the worst part being putting the wires through afterwards. These wires were staples taken from the middle of magazines as we had no proper gold wires, and we bent them to the required shape and put a bead on the end. Astonishing as it may seem, my ears did not go too bad, and a dab of spirit soon put them right once I had had them done. Then my brother, on one of his rare visits, brought me my first pair of earrings. They were little gold sleepers, and I really treasured them. My ears are as well done as any jeweller today does them, and both are level, but I would not recommend anyone to have their ears done as I had mine done. With us, necessity was the mother of invention.

While I was at Rampton I recall the first death of someone I knew well: a girl called Babs. She was younger than me, and used to play up a lot and was often on the isolation block. On this ward calomel was often used as a punishment. It was only given under a doctor's supervision, and Babs had been given this purgative often, and the following morning a dose of Epsom salts. One morning the Epsom salts were overlooked, and as a result little Babs died. Who was to blame? We never found out, but rumour among the girls said the doctors at the hospital where she died said her intestines were in a terrible mess. Babs had no one to come forward to ask questions, so it just passed over, and we, the girls, mourned her passing, as we had liked her, and we gave of the little we had towards a wreath for her.

Time passed and in comparison with the average stay on the block wards I was not on B3 very long. I was transferred to a villa, where the wards were a little more free. There were no bars on the windows, though they were blocked and did not open very far. The ward I was put on was called 'The Oaks', and was supposed to be for the younger girls. It had a very good sister, the best one in the entire institution as far as the girls were concerned – Sister Carter. The villas looked like large houses, and the doors were left open when there were enough staff. There were gardens to each ward, but surrounding the complete compound was a fifteen-foot wall. The ward was quite pleasant inside, and had a recreation room, not, as one would think, with games and so on, but a room where we sat and knitted, played cards, danced or just sat and talked.

Unfortunately the girls on this ward were very cliquey and did not welcome a new face. One of these girls was called Madge. She was really nasty to me and I was desperately unhappy. My stay on this villa was so short I cannot recall a lot about it, but I do remember who finally got me down. It was Mrs Meadows, who had been telling me to pull myself together and fit in or go back to the blocks as I was not wanted on this ward. This confirmed what I already felt. I started crying, so this wretched nurse locked me in a room and told Sister I'd threatened her. I don't know if this was true or not, but I doubt it, as it was not the sort of thing I did since the consequences were pretty grim. Anyway, I was sent back to B3. I felt a complete failure and very depressed. I will never get away from this place now, I thought, I'll be here for ever. What a dreadful thought.

Sister Sweetman was very kind, but did rub salt in my wounds by saying she did not think I should have gone to the villas in the first place. On top of coming back to this ward, I had no privileges, and to make things worse, I got a letter from Mother telling me what a fool I was. Anyhow, things passed, but I did not really settle for ages, and after a row with one of the girls I smashed some windows and was sent to the isolation ward again. I was not hit this time, but I still did not find it any better, and even after twenty-odd years, when writing about the isolation ward, I can still feel as though I'm back on it. Until this time I did not realize what an effect the isolation block had had on me. I find it very difficult to write this passage.

Perhaps it was because, once the doors were shut, you could see nobody and nobody could see you. Maybe it was the lack of natural light, and the fact that, if this was obliterated, you were in total darkness – a thing I've never liked. It's no use my trying to analyse my fear of the place, as the more I think the worse it gets. I do recall that they cut my hair, and that it looked awful, just like the poor old 'wops'. This was done as a punishment.

Doctor came to see me, and said how disappointed she was in me, and to try harder next time. Then she sent me back to my ward. But I stayed very unsettled, and after a few weeks I tried to kill myself again. I'd heard one of the girls was in for life for having killed her baby by putting powdered glass in its feeding bottle. So I tried: I broke a mirror, and put it in some paper, and somehow managed to crush it down. This I swallowed. When the staff found out what I'd done, they sent for the doctor, and then I was taken back on to the awful isolation block. This I had not foreseen. I thought I would be out of it all, but nothing whatever had happened. What a flop I was.

While I was on the iso a girl from another ward was brought across, fighting and screaming, and there was a terrible scuffle. Of course, I could not see anything, but she got her hiding, then everything went quiet. We knew then they had got the bath towel to her, and the girl later confirmed it.

Once again, after about a week, I was sent back to my ward. This time, I thought, I'll try and make an effort to behave. This conduct of mine was only making life unpleasant for me. The resident padré was a Welshman, called the Rev. Dredge. He was a lover of music, and used to get concerts together. He was a great fan of Gilbert and Sullivan, and had put several of their comic operas on. The next one was to be *HMS Pinafore*. I wanted to be in it, so was given a test. I could sing, but did not have a very strong voice. Anyway, I got into the chorus as well as into the resident church choir. This was a change, and I enjoyed it. We had rehearsals for *HMS Pinafore* twice a week, and it made a pleasant break. There were men in the male parts, and I remember getting a crush on one of them. I can laugh at myself now, as he was really quite an ugly man with bright red hair. Everyone called him 'Ginger' and he was not the slightest bit interested in me, but still, I did not really mind. It was nice just to nurse my crush and it wore off before the concert was ready.

The girl who had the lead part had no voice at all. She was a friend of mine, and was well behaved, and the Rev. felt sorry for her – and also, unlike some of the girls with good voices, she was reliable. Poor Barbara, she was teased about her singing. She really was awful, but she stuck it and did the show. Give her her due, she had guts. I could not have taken the insults she took. The concert consumed a lot of our time, and the days passed quickly. The day came for the first show, the scenery was very well done, and really looked like an old sailing ship. The lighting was effectively done, and all did their best. It went down very well.

Another outlet was created by the physical education instructors, who were women and who encouraged us to play hockey and badminton. I enjoyed these, as they were yet another escape from the awful routine. I was never a star at hockey, but was reasonable as a wing. The Scottish country dancing was more my cup of tea. This I did well. I remember a Liverpool MP coming to see us dancing, and before that we had put on a gym display for her. It was quite amusing, as the MP was Bessie Braddock, and she was a very fat woman. We thought perhaps a few exercises would do her good. I felt very frustrated at having someone like that so close and yet to be unable to say anything to her. It was terrible, but we could not speak or we would have been severely punished.

At the OT where I was still working, one of the girls found a couple of baby sparrows. They had no feathers, so were very young. I asked Miss Barrett, who was in charge of our unit, if we could try and rear them. She agreed and several of the girls got quite interested. It must have looked funny to see us digging for worms. The worms we mixed with a little glucose, and I am delighted to say we reared those two little birds. At first I had to push the mixture down with a tiny stick. Water was given with an eyedropper. After a few weeks they started to feed themselves, and the next thing was to teach them to fly as they showed no inclination to do so. We took them on the grass and waved our hands up and down, hoping the little birds would feel the motion and fly. It took up quite a while to get them confident enough to take the plunge. When they finally did, I was a little upset, as I would miss them. But to the delight of all who had taken an interest in them, not only did they fly, but came back and were finger tame. Looking back on this, I realize it had been quite an achievement to rear these little sparrows from such an early age.

Friendships in Rampton were a difficult thing to cultivate. One had to be very careful not to form too close a relationship, as one could be branded as a 'ping-ponger' – the term used by the girls to describe a sort of homosexual relationship. Homosexual was a word I never heard until I came out into the world years later. In Rampton, any form of sex was considered immoral, and severely punished if found out. So far, I had avoided any such relationship. I just was not really interested in this sort of thing, and I could get into enough trouble without adding that to my lot. There was plenty of time to learn.

There was a girl called Daphne on the ward. She seemed quite normal. As she had been having treatment for VD she had obviously been out with men, but she developed this sexual fixation on Mrs Cox. She just had to touch her, and no other person. It was pathetic, as Daphne used to get really beaten for it, but she still carried on. I felt a lot of sympathy for the nurse, as it must have been very embarrassing for her. I was surprised they did not move one of them to another ward.

I never saw any of the higher-grade girls (not mentally deficient) touch the staff, unless badly provoked, but I saw several staff hit out at the girls for no apparent reason. This always worried me, as I knew it to be wrong, but could see no way of stopping it. To retaliate was almost fatal, as I said before – the treatment for such an offence was terrible and cruel, and we had no way of complaining.

During my time on this ward they brought in a sort of tutor for some of the girls. I went, and it was interesting, as Miss Wade was an outsider and was like a breath of fresh air in that closed environment. I did quite a lot of drawing and we learnt a little about the outside world – what the youngsters were wearing and what the latest hairstyle was. All these small things one takes for granted outside. To us they were a real treat. Miss Wade was a very nice person, but unfortunately did not stay long. I'm sure this was a loss to the girls.

My mother came again. This time she brought Buster with her. He had been working on a farm, and was now off to join the army, and I was not to see him again for ages. Mother now had a job as a district nurse in Shropshire.

As I had been getting on quite well for a while, it was decided to try me on another villa ward. This time I was put on 'The Poplars', 'The Oaks' having closed down because of staff shortage. I liked 'The Pops'. The sister was fine, and the girls were a better lot than I came across on 'The Oaks' villa. I soon made friends. Apart from Sister, there was another nurse permanently on the ward. She was a Welsh woman, quite tall and elderly, called Mrs Lawless, and she was always singing. She had a very fine voice, and sang lots of hymns. Mrs Lawless and Sister Sharp were two good, kind staff, and life was very much casier than before. But although this was a villa, we were still very much under lock and key. I made several close friends. Among them was a girl called Doris, but everyone called her 'Johnny'. She was not queer, it was just a nickname. Then there was Hilda, nicknamed 'Nipper'. She was younger than me, and quite small. Sheila was another of the group, also Bunty, who was really tiny and quite elderly. Johnny had her own room and we used to spend hours up there, playing old records on an equally old gramophone. We had things like Joseph Lock, Gracie Fields and the Ink Spots, plus many other oldies. We also played cards and Ludo, together with many other board games. At other times we would knit, or do embroidery, or just read.

I was still working at the OT, and so was Nipper. Johnny, Sheila and Bunty worked on the poultry farm. By this time, I had become very good at most things done at OT. I made a beautiful doll for my mother, dressed as Bo-Peep and complete with crook. Needless to say, Mother didn't keep it. I also made an embroidered picture of the Queen's Coronation. This was done with one thread of silk and was quite a masterpiece. That too Mother gave away.

We had a hamster which was kept at the OT, and because it seemed lonely I asked my mother to bring me another one. This she did for me, so now I had something of my own. A select few of us cared for these little animals, and enjoyed it. I'd also learnt to cure rabbit skins, which were then made into gloves or slippers, but in spite of all these acquired skills, my first love was still clay modelling. I still saw Dr McKay, as I was doing a bust of him, and as usual, if I asked when I was going away, he would evade any reply. By now I did not think I would ever get away, as some of the girls had been there for years, some over twenty, so my own predicament seemed very unlikely to be solved at an early date. In a prison one is give a time to serve, but for detention in Rampton time was undefined and could last a lifetime.

After a while on 'The Pops' I was put on the poultry farm to work. This pleased me, as my friends were there. Also, I like animals. Another nice thing was that you were not locked up at this job and were outside the perimeter of that fifteen-foot wall. Ma Edwards was the charge hand on the farm: a nice person with a great sense of humour. This was something that seemed to be missing inside Rampton, and it was very refreshing to find it on the farm. We each had our own job to do. I was responsible for a few large pens of hens. These I had to keep clean, and collect the eggs from them. When the eggs were collected, I had to record the number on a chart on the wall. The hens that had gone off lay were put in an uncomfortable little cage. Not being able to nest on straw usually brought them back to lay. I used to feel sorry for them at these times, but it had to be done as the eggs were used for the entire institution.

I remember a girl called Eileen who worked with us. She was very lazy, and left her poor broodies, as we called them, without water. There were three in the cage and they started pecking one another. One of the hens was nearly dead when we discovered Eileen's neglect; there was blood all over them.

We had a lot of rats on the farm, and once I saw the most astonishing sight. It was at dusk, and as I was walking by the hen run I saw two rats. One was lying on its back holding an egg on its belly, while the other, larger rat was pulling the one with the egg along. I thought this very clever. I never saw it happen again, though I kept a very sharp look-out. One Sunday, Johnny, Sheila and I saw a huge rat go under a little hut that backed on to the farm. We decided to smoke the rat out, so we got some old rags and paper and blocked up the other holes, and into one we put the smoking rags. It worked. We got the rat. What we did not realize was that the hut was being used for a Sunday school for the nurses' children. The smoke had come up through the floorboards, and the children were sent home. We did not get into trouble, as Ma Edwards got us out of that scrape, but she told us off, and not to do it again. Johnny, with her droll sense of humour, said, pity, there would be less up-and-coming screws. After that they got men to put poison down, and Eileen and I found a dead rat, and cut it open with a knife. It was bright turquoise inside.

Bunty looked after the rabbits, and when they wanted skins in the OT one of the male screws used to kill them by hitting each rabbit behind the ears with a sort of club. We ourselves had to kill the chickens for the staff dinners. It was a job I hated but was expected to do. We had to wring their necks. Geese and big cockerels were killed by standing on a broom across their necks and heaving upwards. To make things nastier, the hens were covered with tiny lice that bit you. The first time I killed a hen was an awful experience. I was pulling the tail feathers out when Ma came to see what I was doing. The poor thing was still jerking a bit, as they did sometimes, but to my horror, Ma said it was still alive. I felt terrible, handed the poor unfortunate hen to Ma, and that was me finished for the day. Once Bunty was ill and I had to look after the rabbits. What I did wrong I do not know, but the rabbits were all bloated, and one by one died. Bunty was very upset.

Working on the farm had its perks. We used to get the left-overs from the staff food. We often used to get a dish of food to share between us, and the staff food was much better than ours. We had a huge turkey on the farm. He was so big we had to lift him on to his perch at night as he could not get up by himself. As for the geese, the gander was pretty nasty. You had to go in armed with a stick because he would attack you. One of the girls had a nasty gash on her arm from the gander, and he tore her sleeve right through.

Some of the girls worked in the gardens. The woman in charge of this group was no friend of mine. In later years she handed in a letter which could have got me into a lot of trouble, but fortunately another nurse destroyed it. (More about this later.)

Ma was very good to her girls. She was firm but fair, and no one took advantage of her. She treated all the girls alike, and showed no preferences.

7

For some reason, perhaps it was simply physical weakness after an illness, I was taken off the farm. Dr Terry sent for me and told me the work was not right for me. Ma was as surprised as I was, as she had no complaints. I begged to be allowed to go back, but to no avail. I was kept on the ward. I couldn't understand it. I was well enough to swing a heavy bumper, but not to do a job I enjoyed. After a while, I was put back into the OT.

During my time in Rampton I'd been troubled with thread-worms, and one day, in spite of the embarrassment, I asked for treatment and was sent to the hospital ward. On this ward were two TB patients and a fourteen-year-old girl who looked about nine. She could swear like a trooper.

The sister on this ward was among the most sadistic women I've ever met. She was a real 'Scots bitch': good-looking in a hard sort of way, and very friendly with the woman in charge of the gardens. I was locked in my room and given all my crocks: plates, cups and so on. I was also given tablets to kill the wretched parasites and began to feel more comfortable. After a while, I was allowed up and set to work. I didn't like it in the hospital, and asked every day to go back to my own ward. The TB girls were out on a balcony all day, and in the summer at night as well.

After a while I went back to my own ward and rejoined my friends. At this time, the villa next to ours, 'The Rowans', was empty for redecorating, and there were outside painters in. These men were kind to us and with others I used to sneak through to 'The Rowans' and get cigarettes and other bits the men brought in for us, although they faced instant dismissal if caught, and knew it.

Then, when playing hockey, I sprained my ankle badly. Once again I was put on the awful hospital ward. While I was on here Mother and Buster came to see me. They let them through to the ward, and Buster pushed me in a wheelchair round the grounds. He'd grown into a nice-looking youth. Mother wrote regularly, and so did Buster. I looked forward to his letters. They were newsy, and he did not tell me off if I got into any trouble.

For some reason, Nipper and I had a row when I went back to my own ward. I was fond of Nipper, but she did get funny little moods, and I expect this is what went wrong. The evening in question I ignored Nipper and went and sat on Barbara's bed in the dormitory where we slept. Perhaps I was at fault, as I knew Barbara wanted me as a special friend. As yet I'd not made one friend, and had found safety in numbers. As the evening went on, poor Nipper must have been working herself up into a frenzy. Suddenly she leapt from her bed and smashed two windows; it was over in seconds. I ran to her. She had a dreadful gash, and was bleeding profusely. I pulled her away from the window and tore the pillowslip from my bed and wrapped it tightly round her arm. I knew it was pretty bad, but did not realize how seriously she was cut. Nipper screamed as I applied pressure to try and stop the bleeding. It was awful. Soon the night staff arrived and took Nipper to the hospital ward, and after the doctor had seen her she was taken to an outside hospital to be stitched, as her wounds were too bad for the ordinary doctor at Rampton to cope with since they only had a limited medical equipment to deal with this sort of thing.

Some of the girls were horrid to me over this incident, and there was an atmosphere you could cut with a knife. The next few days were hell for me. Johnny and Sheila, Bunty and Barbara stood by me, but to make things worse for me, the awful Mrs Meadows was on duty and Sister Sharp was off. Mrs Meadows picked on me all day, and really provoked me in every way she could. She stopped my privileges and encouraged the girls who were being hostile to keep up the vendetta. It's hard to imagine how this sort of thing was allowed to flourish, but I assure you it is true and went on a lot.

I tried to see Nipper when she came back to the hospital block, but she never forgave me and would not speak to me. This, combined with the rough treatment I was receiving from some of the girls on the ward, took its toll on me, and, unable to take any more, I smashed a couple of windows too. I was fortunate as I only had a couple of scratches. I was taken to the isolation block again. Here I was, back to square one with no hope of ever getting away. Surely this was not all there was to life, was it? Was I born to be kept in a cage? This feeling of despair overcame me many times. I even felt sorry for myself at times, and used to ask, why me? The padré once told me we all had a cross to carry, but if this was mine, I was quite prepared to put it down. I saw no point in suffering in any form, and whatever the clergy try to say, I think that they do not really know the answer either, so fob us off with the idea that it's good to have a certain amount of suffering. That is a load of rubbish. I saw suffering, and experienced it, and I saw no one asking for it.

I was sent back to B3, and was very low. I had lost all hope, and was looking for a way out. I pushed a darning needle into my stomach, hoping to pierce the appendix. For a few days nothing happened, but then the pain started. It really hurt. Oh yes, it was my own fault, and I deserved all I got, but by now I was frightened. I told sister what I had done, and she sent for doctor, who sent me for an X-ray. After that I was put to bed and the following day I was sent to an outside hospital. I was taken into the casualty department, and a doctor came who treated me with contempt, making quite clear that they had no time for self-inflicted injuries. I was put on a bed, and given a local anaesthetic into my side. It did not work very well (or perhaps it was not meant to), and I felt the cut and all the probing. Finally I could stand no more, and went into the merciful oblivion of unconsciousness. After this they were a little kinder to me, but it had taught me a lesson. I'd not do that again.

When I was stitched up, I was sent back to Rampton hospital block. It was here that I began to refuse my food and wished I hadn't. The sister came with two other staff, who promptly sat on me and started forcing an awful mess down my throat. Each time I was sick the vomit was fed back to me. By the time they'd finished with me, I ached all over and felt really ill. I was told later that the sister had taken food from the swill bucket and fed me with that. I realized then that the so-called treatment given at Rampton was a continuous effort to break one's will, either by mental cruelty or, very often, by sheer physical violence. They seemed to want to strip you of any identity or spirit you might have. I made up my mind they were not going to do this to me – I was me, a human being, a person. Non-conformist maybe, bit no one was going to rob me of my individuality. If I lost that I'd lose my reason.

I healed and was sent back to the ward. By this time I had started taking knitting orders for the staff. The rewards, as I said before, were very poor, but at least it was something. Every few years, you went before the Board of Control. These seemed to me a load of old fuddy-duddies who held your very being in their hands. They hummed and ha'ed, read the reports in front of them, asked a load of stupid questions and expected a civil answer. At about eighteen years of age I was unfortunately unable to conceal my contempt for them, and was very sarcastic. This was something that came too easily for me, a characteristic which I knew I'd have to control, but at such times I did not care. The outcome of this particular interview was that I was to be detained a further five years and must learn to respect my superiors. – Like hell I would, and I told them so in no uncertain terms!

I suppose it was a stupid attitude, but I could not see *them* as my superiors, except that they had their freedom. What right had they to detain me? They did not even know me.

God, I was furious with them. It was a useless anger, and hurt me more than it did those intended to be on the receiving end, but still, I'd plenty of time to learn. I went back to the ward very upset, and not being very good at hiding my feelings, was soon in trouble again. I cut my arms. As some cuts go, mine were only very small ones. Perhaps the saying 'No sense, no feeling' is right, as I felt very little pain. Of course, this meant another trip to the isolation block, which was as bad as ever, and to make things worse Dr Terry was very annoyed with me, and since I had a great respect for her, it hurt me.

After a week on iso I went back once more to B3. Here I again decided to make an effort to behave in the manner they wanted. It worked quite well, and I had my privileges returned, and started going to the pictures and dances. It was here that I met Harry. I thought he was smashing, and it didn't bother me at all that the girls said he was a 'bum-boy' (or homosexual); he was my man and I thought I loved him. Our ward used to face the male side-rooms, and Harry and I used to write with mirrors, or just our hands, out of the windows. It was quite easy to understand once you had the knack of it. We used to write the funny little things boy says to girl, and vice versa.

I had now become more interested in some of the tales the girls used to relate about their experiences with men and sex. A lot of it, I'm sure, was sheer bravado, but a lot was true. One girl called Gwen had some pretty tall stories. She was a pretty girl with a good figure and nice fair hair. We got on very well. She was not really institutionalized, and told us all about her men outside. She was very fond of the men, had a boy-friend called Teddy, and so far as I could see was very much in love with him. There was another girl called Doris. Her man was Cliff, and she was really daft about him. If they had a row, she used to come back to the ward crying. The staff used to tease her about him. I never got upset over the men, but I always looked forward to seeing Harry.

As time passed, I seemed to be growing a little wiser, and I didn't run in head-first now. I also saw quite a bit of the medical superintendent. He answered my questions in his usual way – by turning the coin. Once he asked me if I liked the vase of flowers in his office. I replied that I thought they were nice but overcrowded. He then told me to arrange them to my liking. This I did, and I think he was pleased with the effect – there were enough left over to fill another vase. They were beautiful flowers. One of the doctor's questions surprised me, as I'd given up hope of an early release. He asked me what I wanted most when I got out. I replied, a home of my own and children.

Perhaps to some this may appear unimaginative, but I'd never had a home of my own and this was my dream. To have a man to love me and youngsters to care for seemed marvellous. I'd no ambition to be a business woman, as my only interests outside the home are modelling, people, animals and writing, so a home was all I needed. I am sure the doctor understood this. The only complaint I have about this doctor is the fact that he was too far distant from the wards to realize what went on in them, and I am sure he would never have condoned any of the cruelty.

Back on the wards, things were changing. The two A blocks were being enlarged and modernized, and the girls were being spread to other wards. We had our quota. It made a change, as we could (although it was officially not allowed) talk to the workmen. Here at last were some real human beings. We used to manage to scrounge cigarettes from them. Of course, if the workmen had been caught they would have lost their jobs, so again we had to be very careful.

Early one morning I was taken ill, and the set-up was as follows: there were no night staff on the ward, and to get hold of them the girls had to bang on the doors, and it took ages for anyone to come. (I shudder to think what might have happened if there had been a fire. We would all have fried before help arrived to open the locked side-room doors.) Finally the night staff did arrive and a doctor was sent for. Dr Terry came and said I must go to the hospital ward. I begged her not to send me on there, but sent I was, taken across in a wheelchair and feeling pretty groggy. By now the day staff had come on duty everywhere and the sister I dreaded most was on duty. I was put in a bed near the office so they could keep an eye on me. After a couple of pain-killing injections, the pain subsided. It was not appendix, as they had at first feared. After a few days I was allowed up, but was not allowed to do anything. I was bored to tears. Exactly what went wrong I can't remember. I think I was rude to Sister. I hardly knew what hit me! She grabbed me by the hair and called me an undisciplined imbecile. Then more staff came to her aid. I was stripped completely naked and given the worst hiding I'd ever had in my entire life, being punched in the stomach, kicked, and slapped round the face. I was expecting to be throttled out, and as a girl had once told me it was not so bad if you held your breath, when it happened I tried to hold my breath. My God: this sister really enjoyed throttling you. Just as you thought you were going, she would stop. It was terrible, and holding your breath made no difference. Finally I went unconscious, and when I came to I was dragged to my feet and taken struggling through the thick snow, still with no clothes on, to the isolation block. I should add that one of the staff did try to cover me with a blanket, but this fell off.

No one hit me when I got on the iso. I think they could see I'd had too much already. I still cannot understand how this sort of treatment was of any benefit to patient or staff. How one person can so hurt another, I will never understand.

I was only on the isolation a few days this time, and then returned to B3. By this time we had a few more new girls on the ward, and I became very friendly with a girl we called Mat, and another girl called Josie. We were always together, and life did not seem too bad again. There were only two girls still on the ward whom I really disliked. One was the lifer called Lottie; I mentioned her before. She was really evil, and told Sister everything and made trouble between the girls. No girl liked her. They just held the candle to the devil, as she could be dangerous. The other girl, called Nit, was not violent, just a wretched pest. She split on everyone, and didn't care who knew it. Even a hiding did not deter Nit, so we had to be very careful of her.

Another girl, called Joan, thought herself the cat's whiskers.

She used to ask us to call her Margot after Margot Fonteyn, as she thought she was as good a dancer. She could dance, but not as well as that. Other than that she was quite pleasant, so we humoured her. One morning someone had skated down the corridor called 'the fifteen', which was a 'serious crime'. For some reason I was summoned by Sister as one of the girls had said I had done it. This was untrue, and the sort of thing I'd never dream of doing. Sister believed me, as up to now I'd never lied to her, and this stood me in good stead. They never found out who did it.

Some of the girls could be very spiteful. If they did not like another girl, instead of ignoring her, they would destroy something from her possessions, or rip her dress, or, as happened to me, hide some item. I had, and still own to this day, a pair of amethyst drop earrings, and one of the girls took one of them and hid it. Sister searched all the lockers and rooms to no avail. Finally, days later, it was found pushed between the floorboards in the room of the girl who took it. Sister punished her by stopping her privileges. I was lucky; the only damage was a tiny chip on the top, which does not show, and only I know where it is. We had very few possessions and we treasured things like photographs and trinkets and our cosmetics, pens and so on, as they were hard to come by. I had a gold cameo ring taken away from me, as they said there was too much of a risk of losing it. I was told it had been put in the office safe. When I left Rampton, I asked for this ring back, but they just said they could not find it, and as no patient had access to the safe, I can only draw my own conclusions. Two of the girls who were married had even had to hand their wedding rings in.

I busied myself in my spare time, reading, knitting and embroidering. We also played cards and other indoor games. Like me, the other girls seemed to give little or no thought to the future. I think the only reference I ever made to the girls about the future was that I'd write a book and let the outside world know what went on behind those high walls and locked doors. Although I meant it, I hardly thought I would ever get the opportunity to do so.

Looking back I realize that we were completely without hope, and although I never conformed, I think I also had resigned myself to dying there, which is an awful thought. Throughout my eight and a half years in Rampton I continued to wonder why all this had happened to me. It was not much of a consolation to see it happening to hundreds of others at the same time. I used to snap out of my morbidity, as even then I realized that self-pity gets you nowhere.

My friendship with Mat was altering. I was beginning to feel towards her as one would towards a man. I was nearly nineteen and becoming a woman. I used to want to be with Mat all the time, and she encouraged me. Sister took me from the side-room and put me in the dormitory. This pleased me as Mat was there too. One night I was caught in bed with her by the night sister. The sister was, of course, duly disgusted, and I had to go before the doctor in the morning. She asked me what I had been doing, but for the life of me I could not tell her. In my own way, I suppose I was ashamed, but, at the same time, confused, and I could not see how it was wrong. Even now I cannot give a detailed account, and will leave it to the reader to imagine, and I hope understand, what an abnormal, frustrating environment we were living in. I can find no excuses as to me at the time it seemed the natural thing to do. I denied it to the doctor and sister, and got away with it, thank goodness! The punishment was the isolation ward. We were careful not to get caught again.

Then, for some reason, it was recommended that I be sent to Moss Side. As some of the wards were being modernized, I think they were a bit short of room, so it would ease the problem if a few of the girls were sent there. It was a sort of place belonging to the state, but not as harsh as Rampton, so although it meant leaving Mat, I wanted to go. Anywhere would be better than Rampton.

8

Moss Side is at Maghull, near Liverpool. It is much smaller than Rampton, having only three wards for women. Also it has no high walls around it, and no bars on the windows, and no dreaded isolation block. The grounds were quite a change from the block wards at Rampton, having trees and shrubs and small hedges around. It was not as clean, but that did not matter. I was on F3, but did not like it very much, and was soon in trouble and put in a room and drugged. However, not a hand was laid on me, and all the time I was there, I saw no ill-treatment in any form. The only thing was that they were a bit heavy-handed with the dope.

I had only been there a week when a whole bus-load of girls from Rampton arrived. Mat was with them, but had found herself another girl. I was a bit upset and did not behave too well. I would do nothing I was told, so the doctor decided to put me on another ward. I knew the medical superintendent Dr McDougall had been at Rampton for a short while, was fairly young, and had two young sons. He was quite nice in a quiet sort of way. He moved me to F2. I was disgusted. This ward had all the lower-grade patients. There were no girls to hold a decent conversation with as the inmates were mostly elderly, and some were victims of some form of sleeping sickness, or meningitis, and shook horribly. I made up my mind not to stay there, but then, to my surprise, the sister and staff nurse started to talk to me.

Sister Ferguson was kindness itself, and nurse Lamb, whom we used to call Tilley, was as good. I was allowed up late, and my door was left unlocked. I began to respond to their kindness, and was put in the laundry to work for a while. I did very well. But it was here at the laundry I was to meet my downfall. This was a girl called Pins. She had a bad reputation, of which I was aware, but I was hooked. Pins was a true homosexual. She did not like men. She looked like a young lad, and spoke with a soft Devonshire accent. She was very gentle, and hurt nobody, and most of the girls liked her, but it was me she chose to be 'her girl' as it was called. Pins was on F1, but as there was only one garden I saw her every day.

At work I was quite content and getting on well. Sister was pleased with me and used to bring me little things in. Perhaps I'd get away from here. Certainly everyone was trying to help me now. It was on here that I became friendly with one of the other nurses. She was very good to me, but Pins realized what was happening before I did. This nurse was attracted to me. I couldn't understand it, as they were free to lead a natural life, but there again, perhaps to her this *was* her life. Anyhow, this friendship caused a lot of trouble between Pins and me. There were numerous rows over the nurse, and, in turn, the nurse used to tell me to finish with Pins. What could I do? In my own way, I loved them both. Nurse was not at all masculine, she was totally a woman, but did not like men. I just did not know what to do. I wanted both of them, so kept promising each in turn that I'd finish with the other. Surprisingly it worked out quite well for a time, and things went along smoothly.

I did lots of knitting for the staff, and as not many of the girls here did it, I was kept quite busy this way. I had a nice room of my own, not with an iron door but with a glass one – a great improvement on the Rampton set-up. In all fairness to Moss Side they did all they could for me, and I am sure that if I'd never got mixed up with Pins, and another event hadn't happened, I'd have been discharged from there in due course.

I was now beginning to have more rows with Pins over the nurse. She was beginning to see that I was not doing anything to make a break. It was very hard to make a decision as my association with Pins was well and truly a sexual one. I looked on her as a man, but my feelings towards nurse were not so strong in that way. Nurse and I only kissed and cuddled, but with Pins things went a lot further, and I got into a lot of trouble through this friendship. The Matron was an old spinster and really narrow-minded. She told me I was disgusting. I would have thought that with all the training they had been given they would have understood the problems of a lot of teenage females herded together, and would have tried to help instead of condemning. None of these very natural human feelings were given any consideration. All there was was complete condemnation – an almost bigoted approach. To we inmates, sex, the most normal thing in the world, was wrong, and punishable by taking away privileges, or by separating the offending pair, or, as a final deterrent, locking the offender in a room and drugging them.

I was still working in the laundry at this time and had become a very good ironer. I progressed, and was put on the top job in the laundry: to launder the Matron's uniform. How I wished I had the courage to burn a hole in her veils, or scorch her cuffs, but fortunately for me, good sense prevailed. Every chance we had Pins and I would be up in the hot room, which was where the ironing was put to air. The staff used to follow us and send one of us down, and finally I was taken out of the laundry. This really annoyed me, and I proceeded to smash the recreation-room windows. Of course, I was put in the usual locked room. Not being very pleased I began to batter the door about. The drugs given to quieten patients were very heavy, and the after-effects left you very weak, but I must repeat that in all my time at Moss Side I was never ill-treated in the physical way they did at Rampton, and found the staff there on the whole much more humane.

One of the nurses organized a concert. As I recall, it was *Dick Whittington*, and I got the part of the Fairy Queen. I had quite a good speaking voice and a quiet, sweet singing voice. I really enjoyed the part, and although the usual fit of stage-fright came over me as we went on, I overcame it and played my part to the best of my ability. The concert was a success.

After being taken out of the laundry I was put to work on the ward, where I tried hard. I scrubbed the floor, and then re-polished it. I wanted to please sister, as she had been so kind to me. Also, nurse was working on this ward, so, for a while, things were fine. One of the girls had been there for years, and the talk was that her bust was so big, she could throw her tits over her shoulder. This I wanted to see, so the first opportunity I got was bath night. In I went, and believe me, they were right: floating on top of the bath water was the largest pair of tits I had ever seen, before or since – like a pair of water wings. I nearly laughed myself silly, and the girl lifted them up to wash underneath. She was a good sport, and did not mind at all.

While I was on this ward, they moved in another younger girl, called Mary. We got on very well, and became friends. I also began to take an interest in the preparations for Christmas, and made quite a pretty garden scene complete with a crino-lined lady, using a mop for the build-up and crêpe paper with net over for the dress and bonnet. The face I painted on cloth. I was quite pleased with the effect, and so was the nurse who bought me the materials to do it all. Christmas time was a chance for me to be with Pins, as all the wards were opened up to each other, and Pins being on another ward, I had only been seeing her out on the court, as we called the garden. So Pins and I made hay while the sun shone.

This time passed, and nothing much went on. It was a very monotonous period. Apart from cards, dancing to the radio, and knitting, there was little else to do to pass the days. Pins and I had a nasty row over Nurse X, and as a result I would not go in from the court. Nurse X tried to persuade me, but I would not listen to anyone and a nasty struggle proceeded. I hung on to an iron bench, the staff all came, about six in all, but still I wouldn't budge. Finally, by sheer force of numbers, the staff won. I was herded into a locked room and, as usual, was heavily drugged. At least one got away from reality for a while, and often it felt as though one was floating on air.

Very often, out of sheer boredom, or sometimes frustration, Mary and I used to plan to play up, and when they put us in seclusion, as it was called, Mary and I would bang the doors like merry hell, shouting and singing at the tops of our voices. Very often we broke the doors and had to be moved to another room. This we also tried to break, but the staff would give us yet heavier doses of drugs and that shut us up for a while. By this time I was coming up to the age of twenty-one: the age when people living a normal life are given the key of the door. Not so for me. As at Rampton, one went before what was then the Board of Control, nowadays called a Review Tribunal, who knew nothing about you except an account given by the institution. It was these people who decided whether you could live a normal life or must stay couped up like an animal.

At this special interview, my mother had decided to put in an appearance. Why she bothered, I don't know, as she made it quite clear she did not want me home, though she was quite agreeable for me to be sent to yet another institution in Birmingham. This, to me, was yet another rejection of myself. I was dreadfully upset and felt there was now no use in trying. All these years I had fought against becoming institutionalized, had refused to be anyone other than myself; even my bad behaviour was usually done to suit myself, or out of frustration. Now, more than ever, I faced a situation from which I could see no way out. I was to spend the rest of my days caged. Well, if that was to be the case, I was going to make my jailors' life as miserable as my own. To this aim I set course. Nurse X was furious with me, but I had gone past any reason and did not care.

9

Before describing how I lapsed completely into bad behaviour, I will mention some of my fellow-patients on the ward. Bear in mind that this was a ward of lower-grade patients, mostly elderly. Some were the result of a disease called sleeping sickness, others had fallen victim to meningitis in their younger days. Both these sicknesses, in those days, often left the unfortunate person with some form of mental disability. I do not say this out of any medical knowledge, only from what I saw and heard for myself. Some of the older women shook, and had difficulty controlling their limbs and heads. Others suffered from epilepsy, and still others were just very retarded and had to be treated like very young children. They often threw nasty tantrums. Some were quite violent, would grab you by the hair and really belt into you if they felt like it.

One of these was a deaf-and-dumb woman, quite tall and strong, called Daisy. Being unable to speak must have been very frustrating for her. All she could do was make inarticulate noises, which many found it difficult to understand. I had a little knowledge of the deaf-and-dumb language, but could only do it very slowly, like typing with two fingers. But I did manage to form some kind of communication with her. She really laid into me once, and I was scared, and because of this fought back, giving her as much as I got. After this Daisy seemed to be more careful, and even appeared to like me. One woman on the ward was horrid. She would creep up behind you and really let fly. But here again I stood up to it and found I only needed to do it a couple of times and then was left alone. I don't like fighting, but even today, if I was attacked, I'd retaliate. To me, it was a reflex action, a sort of survival kit. It was them or you.

Some of the names the women got were very appropriate. A girl called Connie was called 'Pick-pick', because she was always picking her face. Another was called 'Monkey' as she bore a striking resemblance to a monkey. She knew this, and actually did monkey actions to amuse us. She'd been there for years, and seemed very inoffensive. A woman called Iris was almost incapable of walking and was finally put to bed, but even here she'd pull your hair or scratch. It was pitiful to see her.

Most of their table manners were dreadful, like young children learning to feed themselves, but looking repulsive because of the grotesque facial expressions they used. In fact, at times, it made me feel physically sick to watch them. I soon took to eating in the kitchen with Monkey. The clothes were institution issue, and some were a sort of woven cotton. Except for a variation in colour, these were all the same. Shoes were black lace-ups, and one usually wore ankle-socks. Unlike at Rampton, we were not allowed to curl our hair with a perm, and had to rely on sugar water to keep the hair tidy. We did use make-up, and for myself I always tried to make the most of my appearance and keep clean and tidy.

The sister was very helpful and always gave me the nicest dresses she had in stock. I never understood why I was put on this ward. At the time, I thought it was out of spite, as it seemed very degrading to be put among the 'wops'. But maybe they thought I would get a little more help from the sister. It was true that when you were among older patients, the staff did seem to have more time for the younger girls. Of course, at the time I did not realize this at all.

My mother came to see me on a few occasions, and brought a friend of hers with her. She did bring me one thing I really treasured. It was a cyclamen plant, and I was so pleased, as I love plants, and this one was my very own. She also brought me a new dress, for at the time seersucker material had come into fashion, and I wanted a dress the same as Mary's, who had lent me hers on a previous visit from my mother. Now I had one of my own. I never asked for much, but was pleased to get a few things; make-up and toiletries were always welcome. It helped to boost morale a little.

You had to be very careful with your possessions, as stealing was often done out of spite, or just because some of the girls had no one to get them anything; so I suppose it was natural for this sort of thing to happen. Although I can understand it now, I was very upset when a gold Mizpah brooch of mine was stolen from my coat, and never recovered.

Lots of the staff said I was very lucky to have a mother. Perhaps I was – at least I got letters. These were always looked forward to, even if I was being told off in them by Mother. Buster's letters were always cheerful and newsy, as he was in the army now, and abroad. He wrote to me as if I were his sister, and not as if I were something in a loony bin. He even got a pal of his to write, whose name was Brian, and this boosted up my morale.

My association with Nurse X was still going strong, but she would take a mood for no apparent reason. I remember once getting a nasty splinter in my hand. The old doctor tried to get it out, but broke it, leaving a large piece behind. This festered and I had a terribly sore and swollen hand. Finally, I was taken to the General Hospital in St Helen's where the offending foreign body was removed. Back at Moss Side I was put to bed as I had had a general anaesthetic and my hand was pretty sore. But Nurse X did not come near me. I couldn't think why, and was upset, apart from the fact that I wanted something to ease my hand. I shouted, and finally she came, but just gave me the aspirin and cleared off. After this she did not speak to me for days. I found out later that someone had told her I had been swearing. I suppose I may have been. It is surprising the little things we used to fall out over. It was the same with Pins. We would row over stupid things, then I, in my temper, would go and smash some windows.

My friendship, or perhaps I mean relationship, with Pins

wasn't a very good thing. This I could see even then, but I could not finish with her. I did try several times without success. I suppose it was something I didn't want to be without, but it was to be my downfall, as Nurse X gave me the ultimatum: her or Pins. Oh dear, I wanted them both, but Pins won. Now I couldn't stand Nurse X ignoring me, so I played up. I was put in the usual locked room, but this was for the last time here. I was drugged with little pills, and really kept down. I could not stand unaided or even feed myself. I was fed slops and had to be washed.

They had decided to send me back to Rampton, and I can't say I blame them. Since my interview with the Board of Control, I had not really cared what happened so long as I was a pest. I had hated the Matron at Moss Side, whom we used to call 'Bucktooth', and I had really let her have all my pent-up fury. She got every dirty word I knew. This is one thing I never regretted, even to this day, as she had made me feel dirty. Even when she said good morning she seemed to talk down to you.

My journey back to Rampton was quite frightening. The weather was icy and cold, and another girl was sent back at the same time. She was a horrid person, who swore at you, and if you turned round on her, would scream. Then you would be in trouble for hitting out. It was very frustrating. As I said before, the journey was scaring. We had to go over the Snake Pass. The car seemed to slip, and when I looked down it seemed a long way to fall. I never like heights at the best of times.

Back at Rampton I was put through the same undignified procedure as before: stripped naked, weighed, measured and examined. This time I was measured from my neck down to my fanny. Why they did this I don't know; some new-fangled idea, I suppose I thought. A lot of the girls I had known before were still there, and some new ones. I felt a little ashamed of myself for coming back, and I wondered if I would die here.

The surprising thing is that I seemed all right when I first got back, but then I seemed to go mad. I knew what I was doing, and can recall most of it, but I was unable to control myself. It must have been the very high intake of drugs I'd been given at Moss Side that were hallucinating me. I thought the staff were trying to kill me. I even saw a clergyman outside my room with the communion things for the last rites. I was convinced I was dying: I even saw crosses and heard church music. For some reason, I smashed the bedstead up. Normally the staff would have put me on the isolation block, but instead I was put in the annexe rooms, where the delusions continued. I got muddled up in my bedding, and thought the staff were trying to suffocate me. One night I must have been noisy. The night staff came to me, and the next thing I remember is a nurse sitting on me and trying to get a paraldehyde draught down my throat. She didn't hurt me, but suddenly I just came back to normal. I know it sounds fantastic, and to this day I can't fathom out what happened, but I seemed to be one person one minute and myself the next. The recovery was that sudden. What surprises me is the fact that I could remember the whole experience as though it was all real, when much of it was hallucination as a result of drugs.

Dr Terry came round the next morning and said she was pleased I was back with them. They let me out of the room straight away. It must have been the drugs. I was taken to the hospital for a blood test, and wonders of wonders, they'd taken my old enemy out of the hospital ward and transferred her elsewhere. I didn't stay, and was sent back to the ward. After a week on my feet, I was put back on the ward I had been on before I went to Moss Side. The awful Lottie was still on there, but so were many of my old friends, so it wasn't too bad. I was behaving myself and finding life a lot easier for reasons I was to find out very soon. My brother Buster had got the SAAFA (Sailors', Army and Air Force Families' Association) interested in my case, and my mother had been in touch with the 'civil liberties' and her Member of Parliament. Things were beginning to move. I was now nearly twenty-two.

10

At first I didn't really believe anyone could get me out of the place, and in spite of reassurance from several people, I took it all with a pinch of salt. Anyway, it made life much easier for me, so that at least was worth something. Life began to change. While I'd been away at Moss Side the A block wards had been enlarged and modernized, and we were moved from the old B blocks on to the new A block. This was all nicely painted and had new furniture in the recreation room. We also had a television, which was kept in a locked cabinet, and we were allowed to see children's programmes. I think the first thing on television I ever saw was a programme called 'The Black Tulip', and after that 'The Lone Ranger'. We were not allowed to see the news. As soon as the children's programme finished, the set was turned off and locked up.

I don't know why there was this censorship. Even the newspapers were cut about, with all the juicy bits cut out, so we never really knew who did what in the outside world, except for nice things like bits about royalty or items such as the King dying. How they expected you to remain aware of current affairs, I don't know. To me it seemed a stupid thing to have done. I suppose it was all part of their treatment to completely institutionalize the inmates.

While I was on this ward, I saw a girl get one of the nastiest beatings yet. Among the Irish nurses was one who was one of the really sadistic kind, by which I mean she really enjoyed ill-treating the girls. I noticed during my stays in all the mental hospitals, that if there was any rough handling, the Irish nurses seemed to have a natural inclination towards it. I say this without bias, only from observation of who the ones were who enjoyed hurting other people, and it certainly did not apply to all the Irish nurses I met. The day in question, Winnie, one of the girls, was fed up, and as she was likely to smash windows in her depression, another girl called the Irish nurse. Instead of talking to Winnie, she just grabbed her arm and twisted it up her back. Of course, Winnie struggled, the Irish nurse blew the whistle that staff carry for emergencies, and other staff came from nowhere. Winnie was hit in the mouth, her hair was pulled out in handfuls. She was kicked and punched all over her body. This was an unprovoked attack on this girl, and all we could do was stand and watch. One girl who shouted at the staff, and called them cruel bastards, was given the same treatment and, like Winnie, was taken to the isolation block, where she received further ill-treatment.

What could we do? We had no redress, as the staff in the offices who would receive complaints had all worked on the wards themselves, and some had probably done the same to other girls. We couldn't write home and complain, as our letters were read. Anyway, some girls had no relations to write to. If we told the medical superintendent, we got trouble from the ward staff. The Matron was not much use either. The only staff who did take notice always left. There were quite a few nurses who left because they could not cope with the severe treatment given to the girls. I have to say that some of the girls were very tough, and I did see one of the lower-grade girls go for one of the nurses. It was nasty, particularly as this one was one of the nicer nurses, but needless to say, the girl got the worst end of it, though not from the nurse she went for. As I write about this treatment, I cannot understand how or why it was allowed. We were supposed to be mentally deficient and not responsible for our actions, so should have been helped, not ill-treated. It made a complete mockery of the vocation these so-called nurses were representing. When I look back on all that went on at Rampton, I wonder how anyone came through sane. Today, when I read in the papers of anyone sent there, I feel desperately sorry for them, whatever they've done. Prison is preferable to Rampton. I don't know if things are any better now. At least they cannot be worse.

When I went on to the new ward, the doctors had started giving a form of treatment to about three girls. This was the drug largactol. It was new, and I suppose a start in the right direction, and was the only drug apart from paraldehyde that I saw given. The doctors never seemed to analyse the girls, like they do today. You only saw a doctor if you asked to, or if your privileges were stopped. It was the same with most of the staff. No one seemed to care, and as long as you were no trouble, you were almost ignored. I often wondered why there were keys for the taps. Was it a method to prevent you from drowning, or an economy measure, or just another method of degrading a person?

When a nurse died, we were expected to contribute towards a wreath, out of our own few pennies a month, even if we did not like the person. Also, if a nurse retired, we were to do the same. It was most unwise to say no. I was still progressing, as the powers-that-be call it. I think I was beginning to realize it was the only thing to do. It wasn't easy, as by cooperating I was finding it harder going with the girls. They began to call me 'Lady Shit' again. Then, to complicate things, they sent Pins back to Rampton from Moss Side. I was as soft on her as ever, and was glad she was back. Here, again, she was almost my downfall. Pins didn't seem to be able to keep to one girl if another made up to her, and there were a lot of pretty girls on the ward she was put on. They decided to keep us apart.

To give credit where it is due, they did the right thing, although I didn't think so at the time. When Pins and I had rows, I used to get upset, as we only saw one another on the exercise court. Sister used to try and tell me not to throw my chances away on her, and I did get put in my room once over her, after I threatened to smash the windows. But after I was let out I tried to see sense, not too successfully at first. They transferred Pins to a villa, and she went with another girl called Irene. I wrote her a filthy letter, using every dirty word I knew, and the letter got into the hands of one of the staff, the woman in charge of the gardens, who brought it back to the ward. God bless Nurse Thomas, who destroyed it and saved me from getting into a row. Had she not, I'd have been sent on to the isolation block. As it was, she got into trouble for doing this for me. To her I shall always be grateful. Nurse Thomas was good to all the girls, and all the time I knew her, she never reported anyone, but she was one of the few.

After this I really gave up with Pins. I knew when I was beaten, so carried on taking the chance I'd been given by being transferred to a villa. This paid off, as the authorities were now under pressure about me.

The SAAFA representative from Salop had come to see me with my mother, and could see no reason for my being there. Also the then MP for the Wrekin was in on it. I think it was Bill Yates. The Home Office did not like too many outsiders looking into Rampton, but as far as I was concerned it was a case of the more the merrier. As a result of this interest being taken in me, I was transferred to a villa, 'The Laurels' this time. All the villas, bar two, had the names of trees, and going down from 'The Laurels' were 'The Maples', 'The Oaks', 'The Poplars' (the ward I had been on before going to Moss Side), 'The Rowans' (Pins was on there), and after that the hospital ward, and then the old villa, a ward for really retarded patients which had a wall round so they could not mix with other villas. Surrounding all these wards was the fifteen-foot wall with its deep ditch either side. It was very hard to get over, and you could be seen if you got near it, although one or two did make it. Usually one of the girls would split on anyone who tried, so I never did. Pins and another girl got over it once, and got away. They found a boat and rowed across the River Trent, and were finally caught in Lincoln. The usual punishment for absconding was three weeks or more on the isolation block.

Now back to my new ward: the sister on here was okay if she

liked you. I was lucky and got on all right with her. She was friendly with another sister on the block wards, and one of the nurses was dotty about her. We called her Totty, and she was rather sweet in spite of her dotty infatuation. Gwen was a girl on this ward: she was quite nice, but like us all had her faults. She liked to be the 'big girl', as we called them – they usually had a lot of respect from the other girls, because they were either good fighters, or were well in with the staff, or because, in extreme cases, the staff were not too happy to cross them. Gwen was a good fighter, and had a big mouth. Then there was Alice. She was Irish, and really nice. There was also Barbara. She was sweet on me, and I liked her, but not in the same way as Pins.

Some of the girls were not my cup of tea at all. There were the two Roses, who had a sexual friendship and were always at it in the coat cupboard. Fair enough! Each to his own, I was no saint. But they would scream at you if you disturbed them, and both of them were spiteful and stole if they could. Oh, of course, and there was Nit Smith. She was a bitch, and would tell the staff if she saw you doing anything. If we wanted a sly smoke, we had to look out for Nit. We used to get lights from the sun with a magnifying glass, and smoke out on the fire escape.

I was put to work in the big kitchens. At first I was put on doing the potatoes, which was horrid work, but I stuck it out and was finally put on the food boilers. These were huge things in which the porridge or puddings, potatoes and vegetables were cooked. We had to keep them nice and clean. There was a chef in charge, and a skinny little man we called Baldy. We used to take the Micky out of him, as he didn't wear trousers under his white cotton ones, and when he bent down, you could see his balls – he looked really comical. I don't know whether he knew how much we could see, but it was good for a laugh.

Christmas came while I was working in these kitchens, and as we were allowed to smoke at this time only, I would do a few spuds and stop for a fag. I soon got into trouble for this. Marie, a friend of mine, and I had a whale of a time. We took advantage of the fact that they eased up on the girls at this festivity. We danced on the tables and flirted with the workmen who were in mending the boilers, and surprisingly got away with it. I did not last long in this job, though the reason I was taken out was unjust. I was cleaning the boiler, and the tap on the bottom was blocked, so I put my finger in to try and unblock it. Not thinking, I turned the tap, and by so doing nearly cut my finger off. The staff said I did it on purpose, the stupid things. I did it quite without thinking. Anyhow, I was removed from the kitchens for good, not that I minded. I did not like that sort of work as you always felt dirty.

After my finger healed, I was put to work on the ward. I had to clean a dormitory, which was quite pleasant, and I got on okay. The sister did not worry us as long as the work was done reasonably. I was on ward work for a few months. We used to go on to the fire escape and smoke. As we lit the cigarettes with the magnifying glass, it only worked when the sun was out, so we could only smoke on sunny days. I'm sure Sister knew, but she never said anything. After a while I was put on a staff section to work. I had a corridor to clean, and a couple of small rooms. Pat, who was on the blocks with me, was working here as well. Also another girl, Louie, who was the pet of the sister in charge. This girl could do as she liked, and no one dared say anything, or Sister Webster would be at us, so we tried to keep out of her way. It was quite nice working up there, as you were not locked up.

Another girl from our villa worked there. She was very nice and was called Dorothy. While we were there, her boyfriend ran away with another lad. We knew him as Frank Ellis, though he also used the name Mitchell. He seemed a very quiet man, but after he went off he took an axe to an old couple, got called the 'Mad Axeman', and was later sent to Broadmoor. Dorothy was upset, and we couldn't believe he could have done such a thing. I think it was dreadful, as you just never knew who you were mixed up with. There was no segregation at all, and your best friend could be a killer, or your boyfriend a rapist. To me it seemed all wrong that non-criminals should be mixed with really tough ones.

Life appeared to be looking up. I had been promised I would

be going away soon, and people were looking into my case. At last I felt something was being done and that all I had to do was behave. It was not always easy when you were getting on, as some of the girls were envious, and you can't blame them. But it made it tough at times, especially when you had to take physical violence from some of the girls. Gwen and I were quite good pals, but in spite of this, when she realized I was going away, she gave me a good hiding. This I took, whereas normally I would have retaliated. The worst thing about this particular incident was that Mrs Meadows was on duty this day, and put me in a locked room even though I had done nothing. This nurse showed her dislike of me quite openly, which made things very hard for me, as I had to be so careful now.

One day, as I was on my way to work, there were two girls out on the roof. They were two I knew: Pamela and Doreen. They had got up by the laundry roof, and had worked their way up to the front entrance roof. There were reporters there, and Pam and Doreen were hurling slates down at everyone. The fire engine was there, and some of the screws had climbed up to try to get them down. The two girls were up there nearly all day. They finally came down when the staff had promised they'd not hit them. They did not get hit, but they did spend over *six months* on the isolation block!

I was still working on the staff section, and one day, for some reason, I had words with Sister Webster's pet, Louie. I came off the worse. Sister Webster slapped me round the face, but in so doing caught me with her ring on the eye, which went black. I was furious, and so frustrated. I dared not retaliate, as the staff would half-kill me. So I went to Pat. She was fed up too and we decided to run away. We waited until after tea, so as not to be missed too quickly, as the staff might think for a while that we were back on the ward. I had my Rangers uniform with me (having been a Ranger since they started at Rampton, two months before), and put the skirt on. Pat put on a wind-cheater, and off we went. We crept down along the farm wall, and finally made it to the road.

By this time we had been missed, and the 'state car', as we

called it, was out looking for us. We saw this going slowly down the road, so took to the fields. It had started to rain quite heavily, and Pat and I were getting wet, so we sheltered under a hedge. After a bit we decided to try and get a lift out of the area. We made our way towards the road, which we could see in the distance. As we went some gipsies saw us, and so we thought we'd better get out of the way quickly. Arriving at the road, we saw a car approaching. Grand, we thought, a chance of a lift. The car was getting very close now, and when it was too late to do anything, horror of horrors, there were two policemen in it, and they had realized who we were!

We ran. They stopped the car and followed us. Down the field we ran. Pat tried to hide in a ditch and I made for the corn, which was growing up. I heard the policeman get Pat, and the next thing I knew I was caught too. Pat had been in the ditch, which was full of water, and as she stood up I had to laugh: her knickers, which had elastic in the legs, had filled with water and looked like balloons. Poor Pat, she didn't know where to put herself, but it really was funny. The police took us back to Rampton, and on the way I managed to scrounge a fag off them. I showed them my black eye, but there was nothing they could do, and Pat was too scared to say anything as she was frightened of getting a bashing when we were put on the isolation block.

On the iso I expected a hiding, but it never came. In fact, the usual punishment was to be put down the double doors, with no bedding. Here, too, was a surprise. We were put into the top rooms, and given blankets and sheets. I realized it was because I was having my case looked into with a view to going home, so they were being very careful with me. I did complain about Sister Webster hitting me, and my eye was still black, but as before Pat was too yellow to support my story. We were only on the isolation a few weeks, and not hurt at all. Actually, they were very good to me, and even gave me books to read and let me out in the recreation room. After this, both Pat and I were sent on to the blocks. We did ward work but were not allowed any privileges for quite a time.

Christmas came round again and here I got my own back on

Pat for not having backed me up. She gave me some chocolate finger biscuits to look after for her, and I ate nearly all of them. Perhaps it was a nasty action, but I felt justice had been done. I was on the blocks for ten months. This was exceptional treatment, as usually a runaway was kept for years behind bars. I then went back to the Laurels, and for a while worked in the laundry. Then, once again, I was put on a staff wing, this time over the other side in what they called the sick bay. There was also a flat where the school teacher who took our classes lived. This I had to keep clean and I also had to wait on her.

All this time I was being visited by different folk. I don't know who they all were, but one was a lady from the SAAFA and the Council for Civil Liberties was helping. My local MP was also very good. On top of that, I got a letter out to Lord Chief Justice Goddard to complain at being detained. My mother and Buster had been trying all ways to get me out, but I think Buster's being in the army did the most good in the end, as they had a large organization behind them. I do acknowledge and thank all who helped: to them I shall always be grateful.

Life was much easier. Dr McKay sent for me, and verified that I was really going home. This was marvellous, and I was very excited, though still not sure when it would happen. About this time there had been some publicity about Rampton. Two newspapers were involved, and the year was 1956 or 1957 – I'm not sure which. The two papers were the *News of the World* and, as it was then, the *Empire News*, I think. Grafton Green was the man on our side, and Chris Chataway was for the *News of the World*. I think I have this right, though if anyone wants to check there would be no difficulty. Exactly what was going on I'm not sure. Rumour had it that relations of one of the girls had told the papers of ill-treatment. We were not, of course, allowed to see the write-ups, so I cannot be certain. Anyhow, the place was swarming with newsmen, and we were told not to say anything out of place.

A hockey match was put on for them, and a whole lot of other bull! How stupid these newspaper reporters were, I do not know, but I do know that the institution fooled the *News of the*

World, but not the *Empire News.* Really it was a farce, as they saw nothing that the staff did not want them to see.

While the reporters were on the hockey field, I went up and asked Dr McKay, who naturally was acting as host, when I was going home. He told the reporter I would be going home very soon, but still gave no date, so I had to be content with that.

At the time, my friend Johnny had gone away into service, but did not stay as the people exploited her, so she arrived back at Rampton. Several girls did go into private service, but I don't think I would have liked it as I am sure one would have been made to work all hours. I know Johnny said she had to work all hours of the day and night, and for her to complain it must have been hard as she was a hard worker. Another girl called Dorothy went into service. She was lucky, and had a good boss and finally was released. Usually the girls were released on what was called 'licence'. This could be for one or two years, and after that they were free.

The weeks were passing, and we were now into the spring. I was still on the residence, and Pins was working on there as well. But, by now, I had learnt my lesson, and had very little to do with her. I did not want my chance of getting away to be mucked up again. She did start chasing after me, but I held out. One morning I was sent for by Dr McKay. He was able to give me a date when I would leave. It was only two weeks away, and the excitement was terrific. I could hardly contain myself, and work went up the spout. I used to go up to the gym instructors' room to talk and smoke cigarettes. Just before I left, there was a hockey match, and after the game I had to present a bouquet of flowers to the medical superintendent's wife. This was supposed to be a great honour for me – you know what I mean, sort of royalty. But if it made anyone feel good, I did not mind.

Before I could leave Rampton, I had to have some new clothing, and had to go to the sewing room to be measured up for undies and night-clothes. The coat and mac came from stores, but I was taken into Retford to buy a new dress and hat. I chose a neutral shade dress and a blue hat to go with the coat. The shoes were brown slip-ons, and that was the wardrobe they

gave me. It seemed very inadequate after so long a detention –
almost nine years – to give you just the clothes you stood up in.
Still, that's the way the state treated you. I was given no money.
All I had was what I had saved – about £1.50.

I was taken off the residence a week before I left. I don't
know why. Perhaps it was because I was so excited. The night
before I left I couldn't sleep. Never had a night been so long.
Finally the day came, and I had breakfast, and then it was time
to go. It was quite funny. Nit was on the Laurels, and as I was
leaving she turned to me and said, 'Many happy returns.'
But I could afford to laugh at her. I knew I'd not come back.
All the girls were at the window waving. Some wished me luck,
others said I'd not last very long. I can understand how they
must have felt. At least I had hope of a future now. Those poor
devils had nothing, so I just said cheerio, and smiled at the
insults they hurled at me.

Mrs Lane took me home. She was a nice nurse who worked in
the office. The 'state car' was laid on, and we went off in style.
I would not look back. I suppose that was superstition, as the
girls had said it was unlucky.

11

The journey seemed to take ages. We stopped at Derby to buy some flowers for my mother, and finally we arrived at the small market town where I was going to live. I felt very afraid. What was it going to be like? How would people treat me? Did they know where I'd been? All these things went through my mind. Mother was waiting for me by the entrance to the alleyway of what was to be my home. When the car stopped, I hurled myself out into her arms. Her reaction was as ever. She said, 'Child, control yourself.' Poor Mother, she was embarrassed. She could not, and to this day cannot, bear any demonstration of affection.

The little cottage was in a very poor area of the town, but inside Mother had made it very nice, tiny as it was. It had a bathroom and toilet, also hot and cold water. There were two bedrooms, a front room, and a tiny kitchen. There was no garden; but there was an allotment up the alley. This Mother used to use as an area to dry the washing. After Mother had made the nurse and the driver a cup of tea, they left, but not before giving me a certificate to prove I was sane. I had to laugh at this gesture by the state. It was no comfort to me to be told that I should never have been kept inside. It was more than eight years of my life that had been buggered up, and not a bit of compensation offered.

It was hard to come out into the world. I was scared of the traffic, unsure of money and of how people would accept me. I also had to get a job. The people from the mental welfare came to visit me. They were nice. I had been released on one year's licence to them, and they had to see I was going on okay. Mother got me a job cleaning up in a hairdresser's house. I also had to get the children's breakfast, and help them get ready for school. It was not too bad, but the wages were very small, and I felt I was being taken for granted. I stuck it for a while, then decided to get a better job. I had no help from the employment people, who didn't seem interested, so I went for an interview in an engineering factory, and got the job. It wasn't what I really wanted, but at least the pay was good.

Living with Mother was not easy. She wanted to know where I was and who I was with all the time. She spent money like water and was always short. All my boyfriends were quickly frightened off, and the only friends I could have were of Mother's choice. Her friends were nice enough, but they were not mine, and were a lot older than me. I always felt like some sort of exhibit, and if I had a disagreement with her, she always told these people about my past so that I was made to feel ungrateful. I cannot say I liked my mother any better than I had when I was a child. In fact, I was still frightened of her. Why I don't know. It took me years to overcome this fear of her.

Mother had a dog. He was a terror and she used to ask me to take him out with me. This proved awkward when I was with a boyfriend, as if the lad put his arms round me, the dog would go for him. I think that is why she wanted me to take him. Now it seems very funny, but I did not think so at the time.

We had a very nice vicar, and I found an ally in him. He was understanding, and did not like Mother too much. He saw what was going on, and often tried to reason with her. Then the neighbours across from us were fine and became really good friends to me. But another neighbour was awful, really dirty, and used to swop your clean milk bottles for her dirty ones. She'd peer through your windows at night, and all the folk around used to complain about her. She had a very pretty daughter, but the daughter's tongue was as bad as her mother's.

I remember coming in one night very late, and the next morning, as I was cleaning my bike, her mother came out and started calling me a dirty bitch. I took it for so long, then flew at them, banged their heads together, and gave them both a good hiding. She said she would get the police, but they never did.

Buster came back from abroad. I shall never forget his homecoming as I'd not seen him for years. When we went to meet Mother off the bus, she did not recognize him. She thought it was one of my boyfriends. We did laugh.

I had managed to acquire a boyfriend at the factory. Mother was not very pleased, as he had been in hospital for a nervous breakdown, and I must admit I was not all that keen on him myself. But he had a car and used to take me out, and he gave me a lift to work every morning. Life was becoming pretty rough with Mother. By now I realized that she was possessive and wanted me to herself. The friends I made she criticized and was rude to, so I stopped bringing them home. Buster told her to leave me alone and let me lead my own life. It was, all in all, a very unsatisfactory position. The welfare people were very good and also told Mother she was being stupid, but I had to stick it out as I'd nowhere else to go.

After a while we moved. Mother had got friendly with a man who worked where she did, and we moved in with him. Buster was still on leave. This did not work out, and Mother fell out with the man and he told her to leave. It was very hard to find another place, but eventually we did. We went into lodgings with another man, whose wife had left him. This man later became my father-in-law. His son was in the RAF, and I met him when he came home for Christmas leave. I liked him, and made up my mind he was the one for me. Mother was appalled. She said he was no good, but this was something I had to find out for myself. Mother threatened to send me back to Rampton, but here those wonderful people from the welfare came to the rescue. I was taken off the licence and given permission to marry.

The father was not very pleased at first, but was okay later. Then I met the mother, and here again I was thought not suitable. It seemed as though everyone was against me. The vicar who had befriended me was marvellous. He said it was okay, and he would marry us free. I married Ken on 25 March 1958, just under a year after being discharged from Rampton. I thought I loved him, but looking back I'm sure part of my reason for marriage must have been to escape from Mother, just as Buster had gone into the army to do so.

I did try to be a good wife, but things were not easy with Ken in the RAF. With help from Ken's grandad, we got a caravan to live in. This was very nice, and I was very happy. After two months of marriage I became pregnant. I was delighted. I wanted a child of our own. On the site we were on, I made friends with a girl whose marriage had broken up, and when she went down to Devon to get her children, I went with her. This caused trouble, for when I got back there was my mother-in-law and a man I did not know, waiting for me. They played merry hell with me, and said I was neglecting Ken. I was furious. What right had they to interfere with me? I knew for fact that Ken had been brought up largely by his grandparents, so who was she to tell me how to run my life? I was cross with Ken for telling his mother. I thought it very childish of him. Anyway, this row blew over. Then, when I was three months' pregnant, I found a paternity order against Ken, saying he was the father of another girl's child. He had to go to court, and the case was found proven, and he had to pay so much a week to it. This upset me, as he had not told me, and after the row over his mother I thought he was very unfair.

Just after this I fell ill and was taken to the RAF hospital. They said I had abortive fever, whatever that is, and osteomyelitis of the spine. I was pretty sick and worried as I did not want anything to happen to the baby I was carrying. I was having all sorts of injections, and gradually began to improve. They were very good to me in this hospital and soon got me well. When I was discharged, I went back to the caravan, but horror of horrors, Ken had had another woman there. I was not going to take this, so packed up and moved to a little village where I went in lodgings with a retired nurse. She was kind, and even let me keep my little dog with me, but then Ken's mother asked me to come back to him. She could not keep her nose out. Where there was trouble, there she was. My mother, on the other hand, now had the satisfaction of saying I told you so. Finally, Ken came and asked me to go back. He had a new posting and had moved to a house.

By now I was seven months gone, so decided to give it another chance. Everything went well, and in February 1959 I gave birth to my first child. He was a big healthy boy and we were both delighted. We called him Paul, and I think he was about eight and a half pounds at birth. To me this was wonderful. He was a good contented baby and put on weight rapidly – too much, really. He was very fat. The grandparents on both sides were delighted with him. When Paul was six weeks old, my mother arrived. She had no job, and no home, so had to stay with us. We were not too pleased, but what could I do? As usual, living with Mother did not work out. She spoilt Paul, and all I did was wrong. In the end, Ken and I turned her out. The girl next door took her in and after a while she got a job nursing for the county and moved away from us.

Paul was four months old when we got a posting through for Singapore. I thought this would be lovely. Buster came over on leave, and brought with him the girl he was going to marry, who seemed very nice, and were we a houseful! There was Ken's mother and grandad, an uncle and a friend, together with Buster and his girlfriend. I had to put some of them on the floors with borrowed mattresses.

The weather was beautiful, almost too nice to be leaving behind, and it was said to be one of the warmest summers for a long time in England. But the day came when we left for Singapore.

12

First we had to go to London by train. We had sent our boxes containing our household things by what was called 'deep sea', and also Paul's pram, as I had had my heart's desire and had got a big high pram for him. We had quite a lot of hand baggage, and we needed a lot of things with a young baby. We arrived in London and were picked up by an RAF bus and taken to Hendon. There were lots of families going at the same time, and expected to fly the following morning, but no such luck. There I was, stuck with a youngster in a room without proper facilities for washing nappies, and it was so hot. There was something wrong with the plane. They told the husbands, but not the wives, so we did not know what the delay was. Finally we took off from Stanstead in Essex.

I had never flown before and was rather nervous, but the stewardesses were kind and reassuring, so I soon began to enjoy the flight. The views were wonderful above Rome, the sky was clear, and we could see the top of St Peter's. I think our first stop was Istanbul. Here we got out and went into the waiting room while the plane was refuelled. It was here I saw the funny loos: they had holes in the floor and two foot-marks each side. How I was going to manage I could not think. I supposed one had to squat, as I could never aim straight standing upright. Here again was a problem, as the doors did not come down to the floor. Gosh, it was a funny do! Ken told me after that I'd gone in the wrong loo; that one was for the workers.

It surprised me to see that the Turkish police on duty at the airport carried guns. They looked as if they knew how to use them, too; they did look fierce. We took off from Istanbul an hour later. It was very hot, but once in the aircraft, with the engines running, it felt better.

The next port of call was Bangkok. When we arrived it was stiflingly hot, for as soon as the plane (an old Britannia) stopped the air-conditioning went off. I thought it was worse than in the plane. The heat nearly knocked you over. To make things worse, Paul had been sick all over me and I smelt awful and had nothing else to change into, as the other baggage was in the hold. I cleaned myself up as best I could, and then we were off again.

The next stop was Singapore itself. Here we went through Customs, and then we were taken to the Parsarise hotel, which was miles from anywhere, and again so hot. We only had a room, and Ken went to work from there, leaving me on my own all day, which I did not like. But I made a go of it and spent most of the day in the sea. Finally we got a place near the RAF camp. It was quite nice, and was at least ours for the time being. We soon got nice and brown, and Paul grew like a weed. He was a large child, and still quite well behaved. We had what they call amahs: these are maids, as it was too hot for the Europeans to do the full quota of housework they would normally have done at home. So you are given free help by the forces.

I did not like it in Singapore. Some of the women thought I was daft, but the continual heat and the harsh treatment of the domestic animals by the locals upset me. They would leave tiny kittens and puppies in the drains by your house and expect you to care for them, and the smell was awful. Perhaps it would be nice for a holiday, but not for two and a half years, which was the length of Ken's posting. I knew I'd not make it.

The first indication I had that all was not well with me was when I noticed a swelling in my throat. I had no idea what it was, but all the time I was feeling very het-up and got upset easily. Finally I was sent to see a specialist, and he said the climate there did not suit me and was causing the thyroid gland to swell. He advised that I return to England. Ken came home with me, and we returned to England at Easter time and had nowhere to go. Paul was now sixteen months old. My mother said Paul and I could go to her place, as while we had been in Singapore she had remarried. But she would not have Ken, making the excuse that there was not enough room, even though there was. Buster also had married his girl while we were abroad, and they were expecting their first baby.

What a fool I was, going to Mother's! She nagged me about the child, and poor George, her new husband, about everything. He was a love, but she was as overpowering as ever. Paul was a handful and was into everything. I needed eyes in my backside with him, and Mother nagging all the time was no help. It made me tense all the time, and this was not good for a young child. I can look back and smile now over an incident that really upset me at the time. Mother cleared out the dog's kennel at the bottom of the garden and said Paul had to play there. To me, it seemed like locking the child in prison, so I rang Buster and asked if we could come to them. He said, yes, they'd love to have us, so off we went.

By now Buster was living down in Surrey in a bungalow, and it was a relief and a half to get away from Mother again. I stayed with Buster and his wife until Ken was allocated an RAF house in Lincolnshire. It was nice here, and I fell pregnant with my second child. Buster's wife now had a little girl, and I hoped I would have a girl this time. Ken was up to his old tricks: off with other women. It did not go down very well with me, especially as I was pregnant. He used to say he was going to see his mother, but would be with this other woman. He had told her we were having a divorce, which was untrue, but how could I stop him? If it had not been her it would have been some other woman. It was how he was: a lot of it was immaturity. He had to be admired all the time.

By this time I'd had enough of his philandering, and foolishly, in sheer desperation, went to my mother's to have my baby. This was a little girl, and I was so pleased. We called her Anne, and when she was three weeks old I went back home to Lincolnshire. Ken was there this time, and behaved reasonably for a while. I had Anne christened by the old vicar at Rampton, who had left the establishment and now had a small parish of his own. Buster came up to see us with his little girl, and they also were expecting another. But Ken started wandering off again – any girl would do for him. So I packed up, and went back to Buster's, whose son was born by now.

Then, for some reason, Ken was thrown out of the RAF – I never found out the truth of the matter. His mother had married the man she'd lived with for years as Ken's father had died in the meantime. Once again she asked me to go back to Ken as he was out of the services and was sorry. Once again I thought I'd try – it was not easy being alone with two young children. So back I went to him. We had to stay with his mother for a bit, but finally got a two-bedroomed flat.

I should now mention that since leaving Rampton I had kept writing to one of the girls, my old friend Mary. We had been friends for years, as she was at Moss Side with me as well. I had now been out of Rampton for five years, and Mary had come out in, I think, 1961. I still wrote to her when she was at home, and invited her to come and stay for a week. She was living not too far away in Derbyshire, and accepted the invitation, saying she would come in a few weeks' time. Ken by this time had got the sack from his job, but fortunately I was talking to an electrician one day who told me there were vacancies at his place. Ken went and got the job, which was as well as the flats were very expensive. They had underfloor heating, and none of us knew how to run it, so you can guess that there were some very high electricity bills.

With Ken still after other women, I felt unable to cope with it any more. He would stay out nearly all night, and keep me short of money since he spent what he had on his lady friends. I was on librium at the time, as my nerves were suffering under the strain of Ken's infidelities. One night he did not come in when I was expecting him, so in sheer desperation, and with no thought for the future of the two children, I took all the tablets I had in the bottle. There were quite a few. I did not count. I just swallowed the lot. Before drowsing off, I tidied the flat and saw that Paul and Anne were asleep. Then I lay down on the settee. I knew nothing else for three days.

I came round in hospital, and according to Ken I'd nearly died. The doctors wanted me to go and see a psychiatrist, but I refused. All that was wrong with me was the life I was having with Ken. I felt he was the one who needed seeing to. The mental welfare used to send a very nice woman, a Miss Smith, round to see me, and they helped to get me a house, as the expense of running the all-electric flat was too much for us. Miss Smith was marvellous, and would come out to me at any time. Once or twice she sent me into the local mental hospital. This was a grand bolt-hole. I could get away from all my worries there, and it was here that I met the doctor who had been in Rampton while I was there. She used hypnosis therapy, and although I had it, I don't think it did any good. It only showed the doctors things I had forgotten.

It was a good hospital, but we had one very ancient night sister who was a perisher. We were not allowed to sit on the beds, or go to bed before she said so. She was not too well liked by anyone, and we loved the nights she was off-duty. But she was not like the Rampton staff, and never ill-treated me. The first time I went to this hospital it was still run on the old closed-door method, and we were not allowed out without a nurse. I did not like this, but as I said before, it was an escape from the reality that was so disturbing to me.

I think I must mention the two children, though I don't want to bore the reader with the mundane things that motherhood brings. I loved the children, and wanted them to have all the things I had been deprived of, especially love. They were happy, and all who saw them said how beautifully I kept them. To be away from them was hard, and it was hard to know the best thing to do. If I stayed at home all the time, I would get so low and not be much good to them. On the other hand, there is the awful effect it has on children when you have to leave them. So each spell in hospital was accompanied by a dreadful feeling of guilt.

After that first week in hospital I came home, and my friend

Mary came over for her holiday. It was nice to see her again, and she looked well. I thought perhaps Ken would stay in a night or so and watch the children for me to let me get out as I was in every night, but no such luck. In fact, even Mary went out on her own. This surprised me, but it was not for weeks that I found the real reason.

My marriage was in a real mess and I could see no way of saving it. Ken's mother covered up for him, and although she was good to the children, I was always made to feel as though I was in the wrong. Mary went back to her home, and a couple of months later I started getting odd letters from her parents. Finally, some time after that, my mother took me over to see her, and I was astonished. Mary had given birth to a child, and there was no disputing the father. The baby was the living image of Anne. I was flabbergasted. I expected that sort of thing from Ken – but Mary, to whom I had written all that time and who had then accepted the hospitality of my home . . . I could not understand it. Her mother seemed to blame me, but I had not dreamed that this had happened. After all, Mary was grown up and knew what she was doing. She knew he was my husband. I saw no excuse for it.

At the time I could not make up my mind what to do. If I slammed in for a divorce, I'd be left with three youngsters, for by now I was three months pregnant again. Deciding on the best thing to do was the problem. Finally I decided on a divorce. I thought it better to bring the children up without a father than for them to have one who was always out like an old tom-cat. The next problem was where to live, as the house was in Ken's name. This was solved by my mother. She came over and as good as swept us out of the house. I did not really mind as at that time I was in no fit condition to make decisions, and so meekly went along.

George had died of a heart attack in the meantime, so Mother was alone again. She was still the nurse, and while she was out I had to keep house. I did not mind housework, but Mother had three dogs, and they were all 'sooners': 'sooner do it inside than out'. So the place smelt very 'doggy', and if you wanted to go to the toilet, it was a case of dodging the dog whoopsy. This I did object to. I considered it most unhygienic, especially since Mother was a nurse. To be fair, it must have been hard for Mother as she did not like children, and by now I had three of them.

I'd had another little girl whom I'd called Louise. She was so tiny, because Ken had kept me short of cash and I'd not been able to feed myself properly. But she was a very good baby, and apart from being very difficult to feed was no trouble at all. I cannot say this for Paul. He was becoming increasingly hard to cope with. The poor child could do nothing right, and was growing very disobedient. I do realize this may have been because he felt insecure, and my mother continued to nag at us all.

Life was grim for all of us. Mother threatened to turn us out many times, and once I called her bluff. I packed the pram and walked nine miles to the nearest town, where I got in touch with the welfare, who sent me to a home for old people. I was only there with the children for one night before Mother turned up and we went back. The man next door moved, and some new ones came in. It was the wife Muriel I made friends with and who saved my sanity. I used to go round for tea, but even here, if I heard Mother's car coming, I'd leap up and go round, as Mother would shout and say I spent all my time next door. I had no life of my own. She even used to read my letters. Materially, we went short of nothing, but the strain was awful. I knew the children were suffering, but what could I do?

My divorce was on the way through when I met the man I am married to today. He was wonderful, and really good with the youngsters. Louise does not know him as anything else but Daddy, although, of course, I have told all the children the true facts. Paul is the only one who really did not not accept John. We used to go out together some evenings, but if Mother was in a bad mood we could not as she would not watch the children. Even when we did go out, I was expected to get Mother's supper when I got back, and she always wanted to know where we had been. I was treated as a slave – there is no other way of putting it. Mother did not like John. I think she realized he would marry me and she would find herself on her own again.

Muriel next door was a grand pal. She was sixty, but very young in her ways, and she used to stand up to Mother. This I admired her for. I wished I'd had the courage to do so. Finally my divorce was made absolute. The case was awful – to have to go into a public place and admit my husband was an adulterer was very humiliating, and to have to explain to the court in detail what happened was terrible. I was glad when it was all over.

Three weeks later, I moved to a small village where John had bought a house. He was not living there at the time, but he put me and the children in. The thing that annoyed me about this was that the social security cut my money back. I think it was a nasty thing to do, as we were not living together. We did, however, marry two weeks later, and my mother found some excuse not to come to the wedding. This I did not mind as I am sure she would have brought bad luck with her.

Muriel's husband was very ill, and he died a few months after I married. It was now 1966, and as the cottage was tied, Muriel moved out as she said life next door to Mother was not for her.

The village we were living in was the friendliest place I've ever known. The people were lovely. I'd only been there a few months before I was taken ill. They thought it was meningitis, but fortunately it was no more than a very bad throat complaint. The neighbours were good and took in all three children. Paul was by now a real problem, so we were referred to the child-guidance clinic. I blamed myself, but this did no good as it was not all my fault. John dearly wanted a child of his own, so I became pregnant again. He was good. I wanted for nothing with John. I had at last found someone who really cared for me and who loved me, and somebody I could love. Perhaps, at last, I was going to live a normal quiet life and be happy.

We had our son in 1968 and it was a difficult birth. This was surprising, as all my others had been very easy. Mark was born very asphyxiated – he was nearly black. I was very worried, as it was John's first and I wanted it to be all right. He is all right, and has grown just like his dad. The children, although they have different fathers, look like brother and sisters; there seems to be something alike in all of them. But Paul was still an awful worry. I just did not know what to do about it. I had a good marriage, and did not want anything to go wrong now. Each week Paul went to the child guidance. The doctor there was very kind, and so was the social worker who called. She is a jolly woman, and to this day calls round to see us all. What I would have done without their help I don't know, for although they did not solve the problem, they helped to make it bearable.

It was about this time that I met Pauline. She was a single girl with a young son called Alfred. He had been a premature baby, and being the survivor of twins, was very tiny and difficult to feed. Pauline did not like babies, and found her own no exception to the rule. This was my first contact with what is called the 'battered baby syndrome'. The baby was really a burden to Pauline – he was a very miserable infant, and screamed a lot. He had a terrible high-pitched voice that really got under your skin. I felt so sorry for both of them, so we became good friends. Pauline was wealthy, and had been taken in by a man who was only after her money. She finished with him while we were living in this little village. If I had not met Pauline, and seen her problems, I don't think I could have understood how anyone can hurt an infant, but I do see how stress and loneliness can lead to this.

I helped Pauline all I could, called the NSPCC in, and the mental welfare, as the poor baby was receiving black eyes and many other nasty injuries. She always told me what she had done, so it really was a cry for assistance. At one time they took her into hospital to see if it would help, but I don't think it did. It was something she outgrew and the baby managed to survive. What effect it will have on Alfred I do not know, but I am sure it will leave some scars, for this sort of thing must have some effect on a child's life, just as my broken marriage affected my son and as my early life had affected me.

Pauline and I used to nip off for the day all over the country-side. We would pack up for the day, and she, Louise, Mark and her little one and I would go and enjoy a day at the seaside maybe, or visit a friend. This was a happy time for me, Paul being my chief worry.

I had another spell in hospital and could not cope properly with Paul. I was so worried, envisaging the poor child having the sort of life I had gone through. It is much more difficult writing this part of the book, as I am trying to be careful. For the children's sake, I do not want to identify them, for they have to live their own lives and not a shadow of mine. For the same reason, Pauline and Alfred are fictitious names, but the account is true. To the mothers who feel guilty about wanting to bang their infants I say this: you are not alone, many good mothers feel this way. I do not think, especially at the present time, that when someone is shut up all day, maybe completely isolated in a high-rise flat and seeing no one, that it is a surprising reaction. To my way of thinking, it seems to be a cry for help which all too often goes unheard. Pauline was really one of the lucky ones. Her cry was heard. She was a really nice girl, and still is, well-educated and coming from a wealthy family. I think her problem was that she had been over-protected, and when her mother died she just hit out at all the restraints that had been lovingly imposed on her.

One morning she called round. Poor little Alfred had a terrible lump on his head. To me it looked more than just a bump, so I insisted we take him to the hospital, where he was X-rayed. He had a hairline fracture of the skull. He was admitted to hospital, and was there for three weeks. Pauline said he had fallen over the top of the cot. This time I was inclined to believe her, as she always told me how she had hit him, and with what. Alfred is now seven and a half and a beautifully spoken child. He is still very stiff, as I call it. You cannot cuddle him as he is not used to it. Materially he has everything a child could want – loads of toys and clothes – and I think he will be all right, though Pauline admits she still lands out, but she is more careful now. She loves the child and he loves her, so this I think will work out all right, but only because somebody cared enough to understand and not condemn.

At this time my young baby was beginning to take a dislike to people. Whether this was because I'd been in hospital and he had gone to strangers I do not know, but he would scream if anyone went near him. He was fine with the family, and a lovely compact baby. It was just this awful screaming at strangers. At least I knew no one could walk off with him from outside a shop. I recall walking down the street one morning. There was a group of women gossiping, and as I approached they clammed up. So I spoke to them, having some idea what was up. I was right. They thought they had seen Pauline hitting her baby with a newspaper. I said to the group that if they were so concerned for the child, go to the clinic and see the nurses. I practically dragged them down there. I thought it was the only way to stop the gossip. They did finally get it off their chest, and seemed satisfied that they had done their bit. When they had gone, I went and got Pauline and the baby and told her what had gone on. She told me that she had been flicking at a wasp. The baby seemed okay, so nurse was satisfied. That stopped the gossip. For a while Pauline was left alone.

13

After a while we moved to the town I live in now, which is near to where John works. I hated it when I first came. Mark was only ten months old, and the people here were not as friendly as in the village. We have a nice big house, however, with plenty of garden for the children. The house was in an awful state when we moved in. We had to have everything done, including windows and water, so it was an expensive time. Although a maintenance order had been made for the children, it was rarely paid. The thing which annoys me is that having the order made is one thing, but trying to get the money is another, and the law is made a fool of. If a person owes money to the Inland Revenue, or even the court, something is done to get that money. But with a maintenance order, if the defaulter is missing nothing is done. I had to find Ken, find out where he was working, then supply the court with all this information before they would do something. Even then, they would rescind the arrears, so the children were the losers all the time. If an attachment to earnings is put in, the man has only to change his job, and once again the law is defeated. All I got for each child was £1.25 per week. Here I think the law should be changed, as the woman loses each time and is left with the worry of rearing her family. (I should add that for a year now I have been receiving the money fairly regularly for a change.)

As I said before, I did not like it here. My next-door neighbours were not very agreeable, and had a son who really made life unpleasant for everyone. I was glad when they moved. Then a great loneliness drove me into another foolish phase of my life. The Jehovah's Witnesses came knocking on my door, and I stupidly let them in. My first encounter with them was with a man called Frederick Stokes. He came in, and being a curious person, I asked questions. I was disillusioned with the ordinary religions, especially as the Roman Catholic church had excommunicated my husband for marrying me, a divorced woman. This, to me, was awful, as John is a good man and I had been the innocent party. So I was looking for something else and was wide open to any form of brainwashing.

Frederick Stokes was a very aggressive man, bald and rather fat. I started out by asking a lot of questions about his religion, particularly about the business of blood transfusions. I said to Mr Stokes that I thought it wrong to withold life-giving blood from a person, and to do so was in my mind killing someone. At this he stamped his foot and asked me how I dared to question his religion. But here he was, in my home, questioning my belief. Needless to say, this encounter came to nothing. A few weeks later a young man and woman called, and then my unhappy life in the Witnesses began.

Each week these two called, and took what they term 'a study'. The familiar Bible was all altered to suit their line of teaching. I was taught that there had been no cross, only a stake, and that there was a thing called Armageddon coming. This was described as a war between Christ and the Devil, and was supposed to start in 1975, when all who were not Witnesses would be struck down and die, the only survivors being those in the faith. I was also taught it was wrong to take blood in any form. If your child was hurt in any way and needed blood, you had to refuse. (At least I know I could never have done that.) We were not even allowed to eat black puddings.

Regarding marriage, the courtship was always supervised, the young couple not being allowed to go out as ordinary courting couples do. An engagement was as good as a marriage vow. A young lad in the congregation got engaged to an older girl, then realized his mistake. He had to leave the sect and move to another congregation. These were a few of the restrictions placed on one as a Witness, but I was to encounter many more. As I learnt more, so more was expected of me. I was expected to attend five meetings a week, including at holiday times. The children were very strictly handled at the meetings, which usually lasted two hours, plus any overtime they seemed to add on. The young children were expected to sit in silence, and were hit if they made a sound. One woman who was very odd had a young child, and the slaps she used to give could be heard all over. To me it was downright dictatorship. Even the length of my daughter's dress was drawn to my attention by Stokes, but I told him that when he bought the child's clothes he could dictate the length. After all, she was only ten.

By now I was expecting again. I did not want any more children, but there, it had happened, so I just had to get on with it. We have a wonderful doctor, and I'm very fond of her, and she has been really good to the family. She is a doctor who cares, and shows that she cares. I had a rough time with this pregnancy, and could not understand why I was so huge. Many a time I said to the doctor that it must be an octopus or twins, but for a while they just laughed at me. I was still with the Witnesses, and the friend Muriel whom I had made at the little village where Mother lived had moved down near me. She too had become involved with the Witnesses and we went to meetings together. John was good and used to take us all to the hall though he was not interested himself.

I met some nice people in the sect, but most of them were as odd as I must seem to be at times. There was Millie, a real hypocrite if ever I saw one. They were supposed to be Christian, but I never saw them help anyone but themselves. They said they were no part of this world, but were quick enough to draw the benefits from it, such as social security. Very few had full-time jobs, and many led parasitic lives, living off others where they could. To me this seemed a lazy outlook, but they said their service was to God.

Women were supposed to be submissive to their husbands,

and we women had no say at all. We were just to minister to the man, and if we had a complaint, we were supposed to cover our head. There was a great deal of gossip, and if you were seen doing anything considered as bringing disgrace to the congregation, someone would run and tell tales to the Elders, as they were called. This was supposed to keep the congregation clean.

Looking back, I can see the funny side of it all, but it also had a very serious side – the intrusion into your private life, even your marriage. If your husband, or wife as it may be, was thought to be interfering with what was called your spiritual progress, you were encouraged to leave them, as God should come before all. But if your husband beat you, that was different, you still had to be submissive to him. The only grounds for a divorce were adultery, but you could not remarry while your marriage partner was still alive. Jehovah's Witnesses are not allowed to vote in elections, or to join any of the armed forces. Saluting the flag is considered pagan, and they do not give to any charities. Birthdays and Christmas are ignored, being considered pagan and evil.

I remember Stokes coming to the house at this time. I had a small room that the children used to play in. The décor was not very good, and some little cars had got under the carpet. I was criticized for this and given a tract to read concerning the care of the home. I considered this to be an intrusion into my privacy, but of course, according to them I had none. One day a woman called Helen came round to see me. We were talking about the coming of the end. Paul was considered to be an outcast, one of the Elders having told me he was a delinquent, and as the conversation came round to Paul, Helen said I would show joy when he was struck down before me. I was terribly upset, and never forgave her. She herself had a son with whom she would have nothing to do after he joined the police force.

Many Witnesses turned on their families when they would not not join the sect. One Witness, called Joyce, was disfellowshipped for smoking, but had a married daughter still in the faith. The daughter had a young baby, and Joyce was not allowed to see her granddaughter. This, to me, seemed very un-

Christian, but these are the rules laid down by the sect. If one is disfellowshipped, none of the other Witnesses are allowed to speak to you. Some of them do, but many of the ones who are more self-righteous won't. It seemed very hard on someone like Joyce who had shown a lot of hospitality to all the Witnesses and given them free meals – for one is expected to give any Witnesses who are out banging on doors a meal.

There was one man who was very kind to my children, but he thought I was weak in the faith. (So I was!) He used to call me a wheelbarrow Witness as I had to be pushed along. I thought this, at least, was very funny. At other times I was called a fair-weather Witness. I was also told I would be killing my children by not being a good Witness. A great deal of pressure was put on me to get me to go on what they called the ministry work. This was when you went out visiting people and trying to get them to come into the sect. We were taught, like salesmen, how to approach people, and how to deal with the insults frequently hurled at us. I remember once going out on the work, and a man slammed the door of his house. It was so funny, as with the force of the bang the weather-board fell off. Some people were quite abusive. Not that I blame them. Even on Christmas Day the Witnesses were out knocking on doors.

As time went by, it became increasingly obvious that I was not having the usual pregnancy. Three weeks before my delivery I went to the doctor. She examined me and called in the nurse. They both had a listen, and by now I was convinced I was carrying twins. The doctor would not confirm it, but told me to go to the hospital, as I was due to go there in the morning, and ask for an X-ray. I was feeling thoroughly upset when Pauline took me up to the maternity hospital, but after the usual prod the doctor told me to come back next week. This did not suit me. I told him there were twins there, though he did not believe me. As I was so obviously upset they sent me to X-ray, where I had to lie on my stomach. What a job! I was as round as a ball, and it was hard to keep still. The X-ray being duly taken, I was handed the envelope and told to go back to my doctor. By now I was really high and wanted to know *now*, so the girl confirmed what I had feared. Twins! Oh, my

God, how on earth was I going to cope! That made six!

Pauline took me back to maternity, and I saw the X-rays, but in spite of my horror at the thought of two babies at once I had to marvel at the picture of them – it was wonderful to see them curled around each other. The doctor said he wanted me in, as they had suddenly decided now that it was confirmed as twins that my blood pressure was too high. I was not surprised, but had to stay in for a few days. Pauline looked after the children. She was all right with mine. As soon as I came out I had to start frantically looking for a twin pram and knitting more baby clothes. The clinic nurse was very good as she knew of a pram and asked the owner to keep it for me.

By now I had made a new friend across the road, and she too was expecting a baby. Margaret was very good to me, and towards the end, when I could hardly waddle to the shops, she did my shopping. We get on very well, and have stayed good friends. The Witnesses were still on at me, but I think even they realized it was no use bothering me now. I couldn't do any work in my state. The hospital kept pulling me in for a few days' rest, then letting me out for a few days. This was how it went on till the twins were born.

They arrived by an induction – the breaking of the waters by a doctor. The first arrived at 7.25 p.m., the second at 7.35, and both were boys. The second twin was very small, and was put in an incubator. They were clinically identical. I'll call them Jeremy and Jamie. Gosh, the little one was ugly. He looked like a baby bird. I did try to feed them myself, but gave up, as I felt like some prize cow running to the premature unit and then back to Jeremy. I was tired out, so I just fed the one I had with me and left the nurses to cope with Jamie. In the end I discharged myself and took Jeremy home with me, leaving little Jamie to grow. I used to go and see him every day. Margaret, across the road, was still awaiting her baby, and now it was my turn to run errands for her. Jamie came home three weeks later. The children were delighted with the twins, and used to bring their friends to have a look at them. But Jamie was very hard to rear as he had a habit of going unconscious. This was very frightening, even when you knew it was going to happen. Margaret had had a son three weeks after the twins arrived, so we had the fun of mothers comparing progress. At times this was depressing for me, as her son grew fast and passed the twins' weight very quickly.

Looking after the twins was hard work, but John was very good, and as they were both on the bottle, he fed Jeremy for me as Jamie was the difficult one to feed. Anyhow, babies have a habit of growing, and the twins were no exception. They are now healthy five-year-olds, and the same size that the others were at their age. That is enough about babies. Back to the wretched Jehovah's Witnesses.

The pressure was increasing. They were pushing me to commit myself by public baptism, and I had to answer a lot of questions from *The Lamp Book*. I'm no fool, and had all the answers they required. I was finally baptized, which was done by complete immersion in a swimming pool, and now I was supposed to have become a fully-dedicated follower of the faith. My old friend Muriel had moved back up to Yorkshire, so did not see my baptism.

From this time onwards I had a life of hell from the Elders and some of the others. I was admonished if I failed to go to a meeting, despite the fact that this would usually be because one of the children was ill. To them it was no excuse. Even when the little twin had to have an operation on his eye, I was told I should visit after meetings. They were at my house nearly every day, and even if I was busy, I was obliged to let them in. I smoked then, as I do now, and they used to come and tell me to stop. I could not manage it. I knew as well as anyone that it would have been beneficial to me, but I just could not make it. Finally it came about that I was living in fear of them calling. I began to pretend to be out.

The Elders had told me I should not bother with my brother, as his marriage had broken up and he now had a girlfriend. As Buster and his girl were staying with me, the Elders said I was condoning immorality. I would have to ask them to leave. Of course I would do no such thing. Pauline had moved away from us by now, and gone to live in Wales, and so I was missing her. Then I was asked to have nothing to do with Margaret, as she was of the world, and at that point I decided to leave the sect. It was not a thing I did lightly, as I had had four years of them and to some extent was a bit scared – not of the consequences of a terrible death, but of the loneliness, for an awful lot of my time had been taken up by the meetings. What would I do with myself? Where would I go? All these things worried me, but I had to weigh the odds. Was I going to continue to live under a bunch of little dictators, or lead a life of my own and rear my family in my own way?

I settled for out, and told them of my decision. Of course, I was threatened with death from God, and told that all my children would die. This, they said, would make me responsible for their deaths, and hence I would be a murderess. I stood my ground, and although it was my decision to come out, they had to save their faces by disfellowshipping me. But once it was done, at last I began to live my own life again.

14

The freedom was wonderful. My weekends were my family's again, to do and enjoy as we pleased – to go to the seaside, and not have to rush back. I realized how foolish I had been, but, in fairness to myself, I was up against a team that was trained to get people in by any means possible, and apart from being lonely, I had been curious. I see now how the saying, 'Curiosity killed the cat,' came about. But I will try anything once.

With a large family, one is inclined to get problems, and I've had my share. Luckily, I have a very good social worker – not the usual too-busy-to-call type, but someone I can rely on. This has got me through many a nasty patch.

Life has not been a bed of roses, and I have not myself always been easy to deal with. I recall that once, long ago, while in a local mental hospital one winter, I pushed the sister taking me to another ward roughly aside, and in my bid for freedom made Sister fall on the ice. It was my fault, but I would never for the world have hurt this particular sister, and I was very upset to learn that she had broken her thumb. I may add I got a darn good hiding for it, but felt in this case that it was justified. My present-day friends are very good, and I have never tried to conceal my past from them as I could not lie away so many years of my life.

I am always prepared to answer any questions anyone may have, as I feel that by doing so it may help others in matters where there is too much complacency. I had my first holiday in my entire life in 1970, but it was a dismal failure. We went to a friend's caravan. The caravan was fine, but it poured with rain every day. We stuck it for three days, and then came home, so bang went that holiday. The next year we were more fortunate, and had a nice holiday, but I am always glad to come back home. I love my home.

Buster has settled down now. We don't see him much, as he lives far away from us. I hope he will be as happy as we are: after an army career, civilian life must be rather hard for him.

In spite of a lot of people saying television is bad for you, I find it a great thing. It brings the outside world to me, and shows me how lucky we are. I enjoy lots of the programmes, even the nonsense, and have seen a lot of documentaries which are very interesting. I find I'm learning every day. I do hope that some of this book will give heart to those who have had the misfortune of being a reject, as I am sure that if you keep on trying, somehow you will seem to gain the strength to survive. If I was able to make it, there must be a chance for others.

As I come to the end of this account, I feel it might be encouraging for those of you who may have loved ones in a similar position to mine to learn that improvements are being made. They are far too small, but at least it is a start. In 1973, forty-seven patients were ordered to be released from Rampton; in 1974, sixty-three. This was more releases in one year than during my entire stay. The system is still totally inadequate, as now the problem seems to be the reverse of the one I encountered. Now, if the Tribunal, as it is called, discharges patients at very short notice, it creates a problem for the social workers and families involved. Here I will make a quote from the magazine *Social Work Today* (3 April 1975):

What if a patient has nowhere to go, or could not cope outside a very sheltered situation? Strictly speaking, these are not considerations which should delay tribunal discharge,

particularly if a patient has already continued in special
security far from his home area for many years, simply
because of the lack of somewhere to go. Too often, the
Tribunal has to choose between the risks of discharge into
less satisfactory conditions and the injustice of a prolonged
stay in a special hospital, with the inevitable effects on a
person's confidence and ability.

This to me shows how much must be done in our social
system. For anyone to have to stay in Rampton because there
is no suitable accommodation in this day and age is dreadful.
I find another part of this same report very disturbing, and
here again I quote:

> We find ourselves usually with a matter of hours or days
> to make contact with families, social workers, the DRO,
> and others, in order to establish in a very short time which of
> several alternatives is the least unsatisfactory. This situation is
> not always appreciated by community doctors and social
> workers who can aggravate the situation for the patient by
> expressing resentment at these unavoidable aspects of the
> Tribunal discharges or may even refuse to cooperate with the
> discharge in any way.

This was written by a social worker at Rampton, and I should
add that the fact that Rampton now has a social worker is itself
very encouraging. There were none when I was there. The
first principal social worker was appointed in August 1973, and
not before time. Secure places of refuge are needed, this I know,
and throughout my narrative I am not getting at any one
individual. It is (or was) the system that was (or is) at fault. How
we, a so-called civilized nation, can choose to close our eyes
to the things that go on behind high walls, is very hard to
understand. I have before me another distressing account, not
occurring in Rampton, but in Broadmoor. This is cited in
Mind Out (February 1975):

> The patient took out a private summons against a male

nurse in which the nurse was accused of assaulting the patient by striking him twice on the back. The case was heard, and the nurse found guilty and given a conditional discharge by the magistrate. At the hearing, the nurse had denied the offence, claiming that he had been trying to separate the patient from his relatives at the end of a visit. Following the nurse's conviction, the nursing staff at Broadmoor, who are members of the Prison Officers' Association, took industrial action in protest against the nurse's conviction. The staff at Rampton and Moss Side hospitals took similar action in sympathy.

This, to me, is appalling, as in the article it says the staff would not touch the patients. This meant that the visiting of relations was cancelled, and the occupational therapy, and all other recreational things. This must have been awful for the patients. As I've stated in this account, I was ill-treated, but can see now how it can go on unchecked. Here is another part of the article, and I thank the doctor who had the sense to write it: 'A fairly senior officer at New Scotland Yard said that they never pay any attention to complaints by nutters.' Then another part says: 'The number of staff involved has been very small, but their actions caused considerable misery, and in some cases, death. Inquiries showed that complaints have been ignored.' Further to this is a paragraph which says: 'There is a clear need for a much more effective complaints procedure than is now available, or even covered in the Davis Report. There should be no block that prevents a patient going to law.'

The writer of this is, as I see it, telling the truth, and should be heard. The mere fact that his account was published is in itself a step in the right direction, and shows some hope for our less fortunate fellow beings. More things seem to be coming out to the public notice now, and television programmes seem to look into lots of these sorts of things! Only a few nights ago I saw a programme many of you must have seen: 'Gale is Dead'. Watching this, I was horrified to hear that the punishment in the approved schools is the same as when I was a young girl. The girl in the film had exactly the same problem of rejection as I had, first by her mother, then by society. My God, how I identified with that girl, and to think it happens in our times! I conclude society must be sick. If this is what conformity is, I want no part of it.

How can I as an ex-patient do anything to change things? I don't think I can, but the least I can do is to give account of what happened to me and to many others like me. I expect others have made it against all odds, but I know how I felt that you have to be mentally tough to take it and come out in a reasonable condition.

Today I lead a pretty ordinary life, caring for my family and doing all the ordinary things I always wanted to do as a youngster. I regret the lost opportunity of early childhood, and the fact that, while I have the ability to do certain jobs, such as occupational therapy, because there are no letters after my name I am unable to do them. But I have volunteered to help with the adult literacy programme in our area. To me, this will be a worthwhile thing, as one must miss an awful lot when unable to read. I feel I must do something worthwhile in life even if it is writing, as this is something that has always come very easily to me.

I do not submit quietly even now to any injustice I see around. I seem to have been born a fighter. Perhaps that is how I managed to survive. At times I, too, felt like the young Gale, and wanted to end it all. I, too, felt the whole world was against me. Fortunately there were no addictive hard drugs that were easy to buy in my time. I do not think I would have the strength to survive that kind of life again.

In part of the article by the social worker at Rampton, he asked for accounts of the problems facing patients on release from Rampton. I think that these must be very acute. Not having seen traffic for a long time must make the fact of just crossing a road in today's traffic very frightening. I found this very confusing myself eighteen years ago. I also think money must be a very hard thing to cope with, as you do not handle it at all in Rampton.

I can offer no solution, only hope to others who have the same problems that I had. With the will to try, these can be surmounted. The odds against me were pretty high, but I won.

I must pay tribute to all who helped with my release and after-care. To my mother and brother for starting the wheels in motion, and to the SAAFA for the great help they gave; also to the National Council for Civil Liberties and the local Member of Parliament. To those who helped so much in the early days: Miss Rogers, Miss Smith, Mr Ward, and, of course, Dr William Hall. Now, in the present day, to our social worker, Miss Downer, who has shown my family so much kindness and help with problems as they arise. To my friends Margaret and Jan for the help with the typing of this book I also say thank you. And to Joan and Clive, thanks for all the help and encouragement given.

What more can I say?

CODA
Bridget C. Downer, A.A.P.S.W.

Noele has asked me to make some comments about her story, and being of a musical bent, I feel that 'Coda' is the most appropriate title for this last section. In a coda, material which has already been presented in the exposition, development and recapitulation, is given a fresh look, and perhaps some new elements are introduced before bringing the work to its conclusion.

I met Noele shortly after her second marriage, when her eldest son was reacting as might be expected to the disturbances of losing his father and accepting a very different man in the family from the one to whom he had learnt to accommodate himself up to the age of seven. This, together with the move to a new home and school, was to say the least bewildering, and the boy was behaving in much the same way as Noele was herself at the beginning of this story; in fact, history was all set to repeat itself. Two factors, however, altered the situation. A wise headmaster saw what was happening and put the family in touch with a child guidance clinic; and Noele herself was quite determined that there was not going to be another 'child of the system'.

It must have been very frightening for Noele, knowing all too well what the system could do, to see her son inexorably and unwittingly following her own childhood pattern, despite all her efforts to prevent it. The literal meaning of the word 'prevent', as in the Collect, was all too true in these circumstances, and it took a deal of courage for her to allow the boy to see a psychiatrist. This is my foremost impression of Noele: her courage and determination to overcome the past, and to give her family a secure base.

It has not been easy. The parts of her personality which brought Noele into the cogwheels of 'the system' in the first place, suddenly escape and intrude into her life when she is least able to cope with them. The economics of caring for a family of eight daunt the most capable of housewives in these times; and forever at the back of her mind is the nagging doubt about nurture and nature. Can she help her children to compensate for those frightening parts of their natural inheritance by providing a happy and caring home? In this she has been blessed in her marriage to John, who more than anyone is responsible for Noele finding some tranquillity and contentment in her middle age. Now that her own older children are adolescents, she can even acknowledge a sneaking appreciation for her mother's problems with a recalcitrant fourteen-year-old.

And what of Noele's childhood? In spite of the well-worn and proven theories of child care, so many basic mistakes seem to have been made by those people who impinged on Noele's life. Admittedly many of these events occurred during the war, before the Curtis Committee reported, and when, as Noele so vividly describes, children were still cared for with adults in Poor Law institutions. Noele cannot have been an easy child. She even defeated Miss Rendell and the Caldecott Community, which in those days was one of the small handful of children's homes which valiantly tried to put the theories into practice. The one person who seems to have understood her need to be loved and accepted was the doctor whom she calls 'Pop', but this interlude was all too short. One feels that if she could have remained with Pop longer, many of these later events need not have occurred. The tragedy is that they still do, and the lessons of the Curtis Report may have to be learned all over again.

Things were difficult enough for many of the deprived

children during the twenty-five years that local authorities had to make provision for them with specialized children's departments; at least the social workers who tried to help them grow up were single-minded and specially trained, and had a certain amount of time to plan for their future. Now, with the so-called generically trained (and untrained) social workers trying to be all things to all men, how much time or continuity can any one person give to any individual child? What happens to today's generation of Noeles when foster parents or a children's home cannot tolerate them? Where is there any real long-term forward planning for our children 'in care'? Many a social worker, even today, must have children among her clients who have no continuity in their lives, and who move from one short makeshift home to another, never putting down any roots. The lucky ones meet up with their 'Pop', and yet when they do, how long are they permitted to remain? Having apparently made a superficial recovery and begun to put out a few weak and hesitant tendrils, they are roughly uprooted and the miserable process starts up all over again, as so vividly described in Noele's narrative. The iron enters into their souls and they become today's problem adolescents.

And what about Noele's admissions to the adult wards in mental hospitals? Adolescent units are very recent innovations, and in many parts of the country this most unhealthy aspect of mental health still persists for lack of money and adequate facilities. We no longer give ECT without an anaesthetic and a muscle relaxant, and I doubt if many of the present generation of psychiatric nurses have much experience of paraldehyde, or of the calomel and Epsom salts régime which used to be the standard weekly lot of patients suffering from epilepsy in mental hospitals. But how far have we really progressed in twenty years in looking at the emotional effect of an institution, both on the patients who need to remain, and the staff who choose to remain even longer?

We pay lip service to the concept of institutional neurosis, and try to counteract its effects by new methods of group therapy, family involvement, short stays in day hospitals, and nursing the chronically sick in the community. Today's local psychiatric hospital is a very different place from the institutions described by Noele. But what of the state special hospitals? By their very nature they are unable to make full use of the modern concepts of psychiatric nursing, and in spite of being run by the Department of Health and Social Security rather than the Home Office, still retain much of their prison image. Perhaps the worst feature of the system is that because local psychiatric hospitals no longer have locked doors and closed wards, there is no longer any secure place in which to nurse the so-called 'acting-out' adolescent; and the unfortunate young people are still sent to the state hospitals as an ultimate place of refuge. Here they are treated little differently from 'criminal lunatics detained at Her Majesty's pleasure', as Noele tells us, and once detained in such a hospital it is very difficult to come out. Not having worked in a state hospital I cannot comment on the sadistic aspect of Noele's treatment at Rampton, but her narrative rings so very true of the old-fashioned mental hospitals in which I started to work some thirty years ago that I cannot discount the rest of her story as distortion. During my years in hospital I always found that the nursing staff gave a much more realistic and helpful assessment of a patient than the doctors, and the same applies to the patient's assessment of a nurse. I doubt the medical superintendent really knew what went on in the dark corridors and side-rooms off the wards once his round was completed.

Noele's story reads almost like a modern morality play for twentieth-century parents, teachers, social workers, child psychiatrists, magistrates – in fact, all those people whose lives bring them into authoritative proximity to emotionally deprived children. It takes courage to show one's private feelings in public, and I hope that Noele's courage in writing this story will encourage those of us who are part of 'the system' to look critically yet again at it and ourselves.